SpringerBriefs in Computer Science

Series Editors

Stan Zdonik
Peng Ning
Shashi Shekhar
Jonathan Katz
Xindong Wu
Lakhmi C. Jain
David Padua
Xuemin Shen
Borko Furht
V. S. Subrahmanian
Martial Hebert
Katsushi Ikeuchi
Bruno Siciliano

For further volumes:
http://www.springer.com/series/10028

Vadim Kagan • Edward Rossini
Demetrios Sapounas

Sentiment Analysis for PTSD Signals

Springer

Vadim Kagan
SentiMetrix©, Inc.
Bethesda, MD, USA

Edward Rossini
Roosevelt University
Chicago, IL, USA

Demetrios Sapounas
Center for International Rehabilitation
Washington, DC, USA

ISSN 2191-5768   ISSN 2191-5776 (electronic)
ISBN 978-1-4614-3096-4 ISBN 978-1-4614-3097-1 (eBook)
DOI 10.1007/978-1-4614-3097-1
Springer New York Heidelberg Dordrecht London

Library of Congress Control Number: 2013951647

Printed on acid-free paper

Springer is part of Springer Science+Business Media (www.springer.com)

Acknowledgments

The authors of this publication would like to thank the project team. Key team members include Arman Anwar, Leslie Barrett, Bethanne Bond, Patrick Brannelly, Lee Deneault, Deborah Ervin, Shahid Faruqi, Kathryn Jackson, Dr. Jeffrey Kunka, Dr. Jeri Morris, Michelle Parish, Diego Reforgiato, Andrew Stevens, V.S. Subrahmanian, Jay Thomas, and Dr. Peter Yellowlees. Without their participation and contributions, this work would not have been possible.

Abbreviations

ADL	Activities of Daily Living
APA	American Psychiatric Association
API	Application Programming Interface
AVA	Adjectives, Verbs and Adverbs
CEWS	Community for Education, Wellness and Support
CGM	Consumer-Generated Media
COTS	Commercial off-the-shelf
DSM	Diagnostic and Statistical Manual of Mental Disorders
DSM-IV-TR	Diagnostic and Statistical Manual of Mental Disorders fourth edition—Text Revision
DSM-V	Diagnostic and Statistical Manual of Mental Disorders fifth edition
EMR	Electronic Medical Record
HA	Human Annotation
LDA	Latent Dirichlet allocation
MCMI-III	Millon Clinical Multiaxial Inventory-III
MMPI-2	Minnesota Multiphasic Personality Inventory—first revision
NLP	Natural Language Processing
OEW	Opinion-Expressing Word
PII	Personal Identifying Information
PIL	Psychological Information Library
PTSD	Post-Traumatic Stress Disorder
SA	Sentiment Analysis
TAT	Thematic Apperception Test
TBI	Traumatic Brain Injury
VA	Veterans Administration

Contents

Chapter 1
Introduction

Abstract Post-Traumatic Stress Disorder (PTSD) is a mental health condition triggered by seeing or experiencing an event that caused or threatened serious harm or death (National Institute of Mental Health (NIMH), 2007. http://www.nimh.nih. gov/health/publications/post-traumatic-stress-disorder-research-fact-sheet/index. shtml; Mayo Clinic, 2011. http://www.mayoclinic.com/health/post-traumatic-stress-disorder/DS00246). PTSD can be difficult to diagnose, but if left untreated, it can lead to a variety of serious personal, familial, and societal problems (e.g., domestic violence, suicide, unemployment). Current available therapeutic interventions for PTSD and major depression vary substantially in their effectiveness. Major impediments to the development of transformational interventions include a lack of basic disease-level knowledge, availability of biomarkers and translational tools, the clinical evidence to identify patients at-risk, and absence of personalized treatment approaches. The governments of the United States, United Kingdom and other countries have identified PTSD as a serious condition affecting many Service members returning from deployments. Many organizations have identified the need to develop new methods for detection and analysis of symptoms and for outreach to Service members suffering from psychological illnesses including PTSD. At present, a large percentage of Service members returning home from Iraq and Afghanistan suffer clinical levels of major depressive disorder and/or PTSD. This book presents technologies demonstrating high accuracy in detection of PTSD signals in textual documents.

1.1 The Problem

Post-Traumatic Stress Disorder (PTSD) is a mental health condition triggered by seeing or experiencing an event that caused or threatened serious harm or death [1, 2]. PTSD can be difficult to diagnose, but if left untreated, it can lead to a variety of serious personal, familial, and societal problems (e.g., unemployment, domestic

V. Kagan et al., *Sentiment Analysis for PTSD Signals*, SpringerBriefs in Computer Science, 1
DOI 10.1007/978-1-4614-3097-1_1, © The Author(s) 2013

violence, suicide). Within 3 months of experiencing a traumatic event, individuals may begin to experience symptoms of PTSD, including flashbacks, emotional numbness, irritability, depression, drug or alcohol abuse, and increased startle response [1, 2]. For many individuals experiencing PTSD, the symptoms may be overwhelming, but can be managed through the use of talk therapy, medications, or a combination of the two [1].

1.2   PTSD and the Military

Millions of Americans experience PTSD each year [3], but the condition is especially common among Service members, military veterans, and civilians who have experienced war or combat-related events [3]. In the last 20 years over two million US troops have been deployed for operations in Iraq and Afghanistan, and experts note that the level and rate of deployment cycles in these conflicts have been higher than any other war since World War II [4]. There is evidence to suggest that the prolonged exposure to combat-related stress during multiple deployments may be linked to higher incidents of psychological conditions compared to physical injuries of combat. PTSD, and Depression are seen as the long-term effects of numerous deployments, with devastating effects to individuals, their families, and communities. Consequently, the mental health of Service members has been identified by the US Government and military services organizations as a focus that is of utmost importance, with heavy emphasis placed on locating ways of identifying, destigmatizing, and treating these conditions. While symptoms referred to as "shell shock," "combat fatigue," "combat stress," [2] or, today more commonly "PTSD", have been experienced by Service members for centuries, the American Psychiatric Association (APA) did not officially add the condition to the *Diagnostic and Statistical Manual of Mental Disorders* (DSM) III until 1980 [5].

Epidemiological estimates indicate that at least 20 % of returning forces from the Iraq and Afghanistan wars are afflicted with PTSD or major depression [6], though some reports place this figure as high as 35 % [4]. Additional reports indicate that the number of military veterans receiving mental health care has increased from 900,000 to 1.2 million in the past 4 years, and that in the last year alone over 400,000 have been diagnosed with PTSD [7]. Among troops still in the military, experts estimate that one in five has experienced acute stress, anxiety, depression, or other mental health issues as a result of warzone deployment [7]. It should be noted, however, that recent studies indicate that not all cases of PTSD, depression, and contemplations of suicide are identified using mental health assessments given to soldiers following deployment [8].

A survey of 3,500 soldiers, who served their third deployment within 6 years in Iraq, during 2007 and 2008, found that using anonymous screening measures, 12 % of returning troops met the criteria for depression or PTSD compared to just over 4 % when using standard assessments [8]. Additionally, Reservists returning from Iraq and Afghanistan reported symptoms consistent with PTSD including anxiety, depression, and alcohol abuse; and reported feeling a lack of support from civilian society and the military [9]. In addition to Service members and veterans experiencing PTSD, depression, and associated conditions; reports indicate that college students who have served in the military have a suicide attempt rate that is six times higher than the average college student [10].

The National Center for PTSD reports that many individuals experiencing symptoms of PTSD do not seek assistance, and only four in ten Service members with mental health symptoms actually seek assistance [11]. The most common explanations for not requesting assistance are that individuals: worry what others might think, fear that they would damage their career, or are concerned with being viewed as *weak* [11]. In order to combat this and ensure that individuals receive necessary assistance, researchers have begun developing new tools to identify individuals with PTSD and deliver treatment. Through the use of anonymous screenings [8] or newly developed applications for smartphones and tablet computers [7] and virtual reality exposure therapy [12] it may be possible to improve the diagnosis of PTSD, augment traditional talk therapy and medication-based treatments, [13] and reduce the stigma associated with matters of mental health.

In the *Journal of the American Medical Association,* a review of the scientific literature [14] suggests that currently available therapeutic interventions for PTSD and major depression vary substantially in their effectiveness. Major impediments to the development of transformational interventions include a lack of basic disease-level knowledge, availability of biomarkers and translational tools, the clinical evidence to identify patients at-risk, and absence of personalized treatment approaches. While recent research has shown that through prolonged exposure to treatment or cognitive therapy, compared to no treatment at all, may lead to an 80 % reduction in an individual's PTSD symptoms [15], some experts feel that technology-based treatments can also improve outcomes. As reducing the stigma associated with mental health is a main objective, given that there are regions of the U.S. that lack facilities and personnel with adequate experience to treat the influx of returning troops, experts note that alternative treatments can help to ensure that individuals exhibiting signs and symptoms of PTSD or other similar conditions are quickly identified and urged to seek treatment [16].

1.3   Technology for PTSD

Many organizations have identified the need to develop new methods for detection and analysis of symptoms and for outreach to Service members suffering from psychological illnesses including PTSD. At present, a large percentage of Service members returning home from Iraq and Afghanistan suffer clinical levels of major depressive disorder, PTSD, and/or the effects of Traumatic Brain Injury (TBI). Studies have reported rates ranging from 18 to 42 % of Service members who have serious psychological health challenges. Many more suffer at subclinical levels. Challenges remain to connect those in need with world-class medical and psychological health services and to de-stigmatize the psychological health process. For example, studies have shown that only 9.5 % of war-fighters diagnosed with PTSD attend mental health sessions within the first year following diagnosis. Online resources and activities, interactive media, and social networking have great potential to supplement and enhance traditional healthcare options and encourage Service members to seek treatment from trained providers.

The hypothesis of this project was that new analytic technologies can be developed to be applied on social media, audio, or video streams with the objective of detecting psychological signals, specifically those indicative of PTSD. The objective of the analytic technologies is to create tools to be used as decision or screening aids by clinicians. Another application of the technologies includes encouraging people to explore treatment options. These technologies would be of great importance to the US Government and the Veterans Administration (VA) because they have the potential of reducing the dependence on clinicians and psychologists at a time when the VA is faced with an increase in the number of Service members requiring psychological treatment, as well as experiencing a shortage of psychologists who can effectively handle the influx of new patients.

1.4 Project Overview

The Community for Education, Wellness and Support (CEWS) described in this publication, is part of a project focused on investigating the use of text analysis technologies, automated psychological assessment, and education tools to facilitate screening, referral, and patient education in populations affected by PTSD, in an anonymous and secure fashion. Efforts focus on three areas:

1. PTSD signal identification and screening
2. Education and training
3. Recommendations for clinical care

While the main focus of this book was on detection of PTSD-related signals, the overall scope of the CEWS project included developing innovative solutions in several related areas:

- Anonymous self-assessment and guided screening tools
- Information on targeting the identification of PTSD signals
- Automated referral mechanisms to:

   - Online resources
   - Providers within the VA system
   - Educational materials

Given the demonstrated high accuracy in detection of PTSD signals comparable to that of human experts (as described in Chap. 7,) the technologies behind CEWS may significantly contribute to establishing best practices and quality standards for the use of online text and interactions as an integral component of PTSD screening, education, and referral activities. It is anticipated that the technologies will be suitable for integration into current and future web-based social platforms including: MyHealtheVet (www.myhealth.va.gov); Real Warriors (www.realwarriors. net); and Military OneSource (www.militaryonesource.com). Another use case of these technologies is integration into telemedicine applications where they can be used for screening patient communications. Additionally, it is anticipated that the availability of these resources will aid Service members, their providers, and families in assessing their condition, mitigating feelings of isolation and achieving their full potential.

1.5   Book Outline

The book provides background information on PTSD and related psychological signals; details the technology developed, the data flows, the processing and results; and a sample system implementation. More specifically the subsequent chapters cover:

1. An introduction to PTSD that will explain the notion of PTSD-related psychological signals, and will also present the categorization of PTSD symptoms, the sources and methodologies used to unify clinical and colloquial terms into a PTSD ontology, and the resulting ontology.
2. A description of the selection of data sources serving as inputs to the system for training and testing the text analysis algorithms. This section will also cover the selection criteria applied to web forums and blogs, and will explain the role the materials from the psychological library play in the project. Further, the data collection and pre-processing workflow before the data is stored in a database and submitted to the text analysis engine for processing will be described.
3. As part of the discussion on text analysis of PTSD text, a description of the general approach taken with the extraction and quantification of PTSD-related signals with an overview of the relevant natural language processing techniques, focusing on sentiment mining, and the role of the annotated corpus. Additionally, the human annotation process and tools developed for creating algorithm training and testing data sets will be outlined.
4. An overview of the SentiMetrix© SentiGrade™ scoring engine, and a description of the enhancements made to the engine and the training that was necessary to tune it for the detection of PTSD-related signals.
5. A sample system implementation integrating all the tools into a cohesive environment, implementing an automated end-to-end process, including social networking features used for collecting data from anonymous user participation. The system architecture, including the data flow and feedback loops, as well as the reports generated by the system will also be outlined.
6. Finally, the project findings are presented. These findings compare and contrast the results produced by the automated system with evaluation of the same anonymous

data set by a team of clinical psychologists. The analysis presents strong supporting evidence of viability of automated detection of psychological signals associated with PTSD.

References

1. National Institute of Mental Health (NIMH) (2007) Post traumatic stress disorder research fact sheet. http://www.nimh.nih.gov/health/publications/post-traumatic-stress-disorder-research-fact-sheet/index.shtml. Accessed 11 Oct 2011
2. Mayo Clinic (2011) Post-traumatic stress disorder (PTSD). http://www.mayoclinic.com/health/post-traumatic-stress-disorder/DS00246. Accessed 11 Oct 2011
3. National Institute of Mental Health (NIMH). Post-traumatic stress disorder (easy-to-read). http://www.nimh.nih.gov/health/publications/post-traumatic-stress-disorder-easy-to-read/index.shtml. Accessed 11 Oct 2011
4. Science Daily (2009) Iraq troops' PTSD rate as high as 35 percent, analysis finds. http://www.sciencedaily.com/releases/2009/09/090914151629.htm. Accessed 11 Oct 2011
5. US Department of Veterans Affairs. PTSD History and Overview. http://www.ptsd.va.gov/professional/pages/ptsd-overview.asp. Accessed 5 Oct 2013
6. News Medical (2010) 20% of returning war veterans report PTSD or major depression. http://www.news-medical.net/news/20100604/2025-of-returning-war-veterans-report-PTSD-or-major-depression.aspx. Accessed 11 Oct 2011
7. Mail Online (2011) Healing apps: pentagon uses smart phones and tablets to treat PTSD. http://www.dailymail.co.uk/sciencetech/article-2018939/Healing-apps-Pentagon-uses-smart-phones-treat-PTSD.html#. Accessed 11 Oct 2011
8. Genevra Pittman (2011) Mental health tests don't catch all troubled troops. Reuters Health http://www.reuters.com/article/2011/10/04/us-mental-health-tests-idUS-TRE7936K920111004. Accessed 11 Oct 2011
9. Amy Norton (2011) After tour, Reservists' mental health may suffer. Reuters Health. http://www.reuters.com/article/2011/07/21/us-reservists-mentalhealth-idUSTRE76K64J20110721. Accessed 11 Oct 2011
10. Sharon Jayson (2011) Suicide attempts higher for veterans on campus. USA Today. http://yourlife.usatoday.com/health/medical/mentalhealth/story/2011/08/Suicide-attempts-higher-for-veterans-on-campus/49808298/1. Accessed 11 Oct 2011
11. National Center for PTSD (2007) What can I do if I think I have PTSD? http://www.ptsd.va.gov/public/pages/what-if-think-have-ptsd.asp. Accessed 11 Oct 2011
12. Pool/CNN (2011) Virtual reality helps vets deal with PTSD. WNEM TV 5. http://www.wnem.com/story/15598762/virtual-reality-helps-vets-deal-with-ptsd. Accessed 11 Oct 2011
13. Gibbons TJ (2011) PTSD: combat veterans can turn to therapy to ease the trauma. The Florida Times-Union. http://jacksonville.com/news/health-and-fitness/2011-10-10/story/ptsd-combat-veterans-can-turn-therapy-help-ease-trauma. Accessed 11 Oct 2011
14. Krystal JH, Rosenheck RA, Cramer JA, Vessicchio JC et al (2011) Adjunctive risperidone treatment for antidepressant-resistant symptoms of chronic military service-related PTSD. J Am Med Assoc 306(5):493–502. doi:10.1001/jama.2011.1080
15. Charles Bankhead (2011) Cognitive therapy gets nod for PTSD prevention. MedPage Today. http://www.medpagetoday.com/Psychiatry/AnxietyStress/28852. Accessed 11 Oct 2011
16. Eric Fink (2011) PTSD a very real concern for Boise doctors as troops come home. KIVI-TV 6 – Boise ID. http://www.kivitv.com/news/local/131120243.html. Accessed 11 Oct 2011

Chapter 2
Introduction to PTSD Signals

Abstract Post-traumatic stress disorder (PTSD) is a medical condition caused by direct exposure to a severe traumatic experience. PTSD is the most commonly diagnosed neuropsychiatric disorder among deployed and post-deployed military populations. Most people with this diagnosis adapt through mental health treatment or other psychosocial support. However, a significant subset develops chronic PTSD, a highly disabling, and potentially fatal condition. A method within projective assessment psychology infers clinical meaning and develops diagnostic hypotheses from a person's writings about self or others to detect possible signals of PTSD. A contemporary adaptation uses anonymous social media texts and postings. In order for clinicians-raters to rate these anonymous social media texts for the presence and frequency of suspected signals of PTSD, a lexical ontology was developed. This process involved creating an expert-generated list of words, terms, and symptoms beyond the standard 17 definitional symptoms in the official diagnostic psychiatric manual *Diagnostic and Statistical Manual of Mental Disorders (4th Edition Text Revision)* (DSM-IV-TR). A final list of 65 terms was developed and categorized into five Level 1 categories: Behavioral, Cognitive, Emotional, Functional, and Physical. The utility of this approach is discussed in subsequent chapters.

2.1 Introduction

Post-traumatic stress disorder (PTSD) is a relatively new medical term for a reactive and highly maladaptive syndrome that has been known since antiquity. The psychological toll and enduring psychological after-effects of extreme trauma—for example as a consequence of physical or sexual abuse, natural disaster, or the horrors experienced in warfare—are common knowledge. Most people who experience such trauma adapt reasonably well with the passage of time using normal supportive interpersonal relationships and/or short-term counseling, but a significant subset develop a pervasive and often debilitating psychiatric condition called acute PTSD.

A small subset of these PTSD patients continues to manifest symptoms that persist for more than 3 months after the trauma. These symptoms define people with chronic PTSD. The personal consequences and psychiatric morbidity of this syndrome are significant because many of these patients continue to experience symptoms for the rest of their lives.

Post-traumatic stress disorder was introduced as a formal psychiatric diagnosis in the third edition of the definitive psychiatric diagnostic textbook, *Diagnostic and Statistical Manual of Mental Disorders* (DSM) [1], although an earlier edition did include a category known as *traumatic neurosis*. In the current *Diagnostic and Statistical Manual of Mental Disorders (4th Edition Text Revision)* DSM-IV-TR model [2], PTSD is noted as one of ten types of Anxiety Disorders. The defining symptoms and formal criteria that must be satisfied in order to diagnose PTSD have changed very little since it was first introduced, however recent drafts of the fifth edition of the DSM (scheduled for publication in May 2013) propose moving PTSD into a new category, dubbed *Trauma- and Stressor-Related Disorders*. Alterations to the current diagnostic criteria may include expanding the range of events that constitute trauma, and adding a new cluster of symptoms involving negative alterations in cognition and mood. These proposed changes are likely to increase both the incidence and prevalence of diagnosed cases of PTSD in both military and civilian populations. This in turn may substantially increase the financial burden upon the healthcare system related to the treatment of PTSD.

Moreover, recent advances in research have revealed the neuropsychiatric aspects of PTSD. Evidence suggests that it is a brain-based disorder, and not—as had been assumed in previous generations—solely an emotional disorder or merely a case of the *nerves* or *battle fatigue*. Coined by Schwarz and Kowalski, [3] the term *malignant memories* is now generally accepted as a useful construct emphasizing the maladaptive memory operations universally found among PTSD patients. Empirical findings from cognitive science research strongly support the self-reported experiences of and clinical observations of PTSD patients regarding memory operations. The two major memory anomalies that occur in the syndrome are intrusive memories and retrograde memory deficits. These somewhat contradictory processes can be resolved by distinguishing intrusive memories from more conventional narrative memories. The intrusive memories reported by PTSD patients are unpredictably recurrent, exceptionally vivid, affect-infused, and involve an experiential reliving of the trauma as if in the present. These intrusive memories are image based (i.e., visual-perceptual live dreams) rather than verbal in nature. In contrast, the other form of memory anomalies include psychogenic amnesia, an inability to recall global or specific aspects of the traumatic experience not explained by normal memory processes as well as the psychological defenses guarding against conscious recall of painful memories, as in active avoidance behaviors. Intrusive memories are often reported to be the most painful and debilitating symptom of PTSD. Some types of cognitive behavioral treatment seek to directly detach the malignant elements (i.e., painful affect) from the factual or narrative information, thereby making the resulting memories more bearable and less phobic.

According to the current DSM-IV-TR, a diagnosis of PTSD first requires that the person experience, witness, or be exposed to a traumatic event involving actual or threatened death or serious injury to oneself or others. Second, the person must react with intense fear, helplessness, or horror. Revisions proposed for DSM-V eliminate the latter requirement and extend the former to include learning of such trauma to close relatives or friends, or confronting evidence of such trauma first-hand as, for example, to police and fire department personnel.

The DSM-IV-TR identifies 17 possible specific symptoms associated with post-traumatic stress disorder, grouped into three symptom categories. These groupings are usually labeled Re-experiencing, Arousal, and Avoidance (symptoms and groupings are presented in Table 2.1). A person must meet the criterion for *each* of these three categories in order to qualify for a diagnosis of PTSD. For example, a minimum of three of the seven symptoms of persistent Avoidance must be present, ranging from conscious suppression of thoughts, feelings, or conversations associated with the experience to frank psychogenic memory deficits (amnesia) involving the event. At least two symptoms of persistent Arousal are required, as well as at least one symptom associated with persistent Re-experiencing of the traumatic event.

The symptom profile for PTSD is highly specific and distinct from that of other anxiety disorders. In fact, some authors prefer to associate PTSD more with the pathological class known as dissociative disorders, inasmuch as anxiety, per se, is not a defining symptom of PTSD.

Recently, there has been considerable interest in measuring and interpreting the non-verbal and affective (prosodic) elements of interpersonal communications. Pentland's [4] model of *Honest Signals* has found impressive evidence for both the presence of less than conscious non-verbal signals, as well as for their utility in predicting important concurrent and future behavior. This emerging field, network science, tries to understand people's behavior by examining non-verbal aspects of their social networks. With the rise of and near universal use of social media, interest has returned to the possible detection of *Honest Signals* from the narrative text analysis of blogs, discussion forums, chat-room entries, and other electronic social networking sources.

Evaluating narrative text for lexical *signals*, a correlate, or predictors of potentially significant syndromes or behaviors, is a familiar and time-honored method in projective personality assessment. As articulated by Frank [5], the *projective hypothesis* posits that, beyond the overt content of their creative narratives and/or communications, people unwittingly reveal many important (and often unconscious) aspects of themselves to others. On this basis, assessment psychologists have used such diverse methods as interpreting responses to standard inkblots, stories told to ambiguous achromatic pictures, written responses to incomplete sentence stems, instantaneous responses to word association tests, and human figure drawings to infer both normal personality characteristics and evidence of psychopathology. Interpreting some of these projective techniques requires professional training and considerable supervised experience. [6] Others have simple objective scoring or coding criteria. For example, the checklist of Emotional Indicators on human figure drawings allowing clinical psychologists to screen children into one of several clinical groups

Table 2.1 Diagnostic criteria for PTSD (DSM-IV 309.81)

Diagnostic criteria	Symptoms
Re-experiencing: The traumatic event is persistently re-experienced, as indicated by one (or more) of these symptoms.	• Recurrent and intrusive distressing recollections of the event, including images, thoughts, or perceptions • Recurrent distressing dreams of the event • Acting or feeling as if the traumatic event were recurring (includes a sense of reliving the experience, illusions, hallucinations, and dissociative flashback episodes, including those that occur on awakening or when intoxicated) • Intense psychological distress at exposure to internal or external cues that symbolize or resemble an aspect of the traumatic event • Physiological reactivity on exposure to internal or external cues that symbolize or resemble an aspect of the traumatic event
Avoidance: Persistent avoidance of stimuli associated with the trauma and numbing of general responsiveness (not present before the trauma), as indicated by three (or more) of these symptoms.	• Efforts to avoid thoughts, feelings, or conversations associated with the trauma • Efforts to avoid activities, places, or people that arouse recollections of the trauma • Inability to recall an important aspect of the trauma • Markedly diminished interest or participation in significant activities • Feeling of detachment or estrangement from others • Restricted range of affect (e.g., unable to have loving feelings) • Sense of a foreshortened future (e.g., does not expect to have a career, marriage, children, or a normal life span)
Arousal: Persistent symptoms of increased arousal (not present before the trauma), as indicated by two (or more) of these symptoms.	• Difficulty falling or staying asleep • Irritability or outbursts of anger • Difficulty concentrating • Hyper vigilance • Exaggerated startle response

Source: American Psychiatric Association (2000)

ranging from *likely pathological* to *likely normal*. Because these are screening evaluations, triggering more comprehensive assessments, the scoring/coding summary scores are intentionally developed to minimize false negative error, and conversely, are vulnerable to considerable false positive classifications.

The manual for one popular projective instrument, the Thematic Apperception Test (TAT), states explicitly that to a trained interpreter, "some of the dominant drives, emotions, sentiments, complexes and conflicts of a personality" can be discerned through a direct textual analysis of the stories told to the deliberately ambiguous TAT pictures. [7] In an earlier publication, Morgan and Murray [8] characterized the analytical process of inferring "inner forces and arrangements, wishes, fears, and traces of past experiences" as a matter of *double hearing*— namely, attending to the manifest (overt) content of a person's communication, while simultaneously seeking clues to its latent (covert) significance with respect to personality dynamics or psychopathology.

Evidence of this type of *inner forces* as a possible signal of PTSD that may be inferred from specific words employed and/or experiences described in communications posted, for example, to online message boards or social networking sites. The *projective hypothesis* is equally valid in the interpretation of known patients' writings as it is among non-clinical or post-treatment populations.

2.2   Developing an Etymology of Terms for PTSD

In psychiatric practice, the clinical assessment of PTSD is relatively straightforward. A brief, semi-structured interview is usually sufficient to elicit the needed trauma history, symptom patterns, and their respective frequencies. Medical sociologists report that psychiatrists often make DSM-based diagnoses within minutes of meeting a patient. [9] Non-medical clinicians often supplement such interview data with dedicated self-report scales or structured interviews, either published commercially or available in the public domain. This type of PTSD self-report scale typically has the same structure: Respondents are asked to indicate whether each of the 17 DSM-IV symptoms is present or absent, and rate the frequency and/or intensity of each symptom reported. For example, a questionnaire recommended by the National Center for PTSD, the structured *Clinician-Administered PTSD Scale* [10], asks directly about the presence, frequency, and intensity of each of the 17 possible PTSD symptoms (e.g., "Have you ever had dreams about [event]?"). While these types of self-report rating scales are the *gold standard* in most types of PTSD research, there are many other focal, validated psychological tests assessing PTSD. Additionally all of the comprehensive personality assessment inventories (e.g., MMPI-2—*Minnesota Multiphasic Personality Inventory: Revised Edition*; MCMI-III—*Millon Clinical Multiaxial Inventory-III*) have one or more PTSD subscales that use both obvious (face valid) items as well as disguised item content to measure the presence and severity of PTSD. Because PTSD remains a controversial diagnosis with no laboratory or physiological tests shown useful for making a diagnosis, the use of multi-method assessment is especially useful in civil litigation cases and in Social Security Disability applications. Stated candidly, PTSD is probably the easiest psychiatric syndrome to fake and the assessment of malingering is often the unspoken second issue to be evaluated when assessing military and post-deployment populations.

In contrast, the development of natural language ontology of terms to infer from social media communications the presence of or vulnerability to PTSD is considerably more complex. The task involves more than a Roget's Thesaurus exercise of finding synonyms for the definitive canon of 17 psychiatric symptoms. Just as

Table 2.2 Instance Level 1
and Instance Level 2 terms

Level 1 terms	Level 2 term count
Behavioral	11
Cognitive	20
Emotional	16
Functional	4
Physical	14

patients typically do not report the textbook (technical) symptoms, their common synonyms are also not generally reported in clinical practice. Rather, patients tend to report symptoms in an experience-near anecdotal or colloquial manner, or in generalizations that reveal some type of psychopathology, frequently common anger, depression, or relationship problems with a spouse or partner. PTSD is rarely a sole psychiatric diagnosis and its comorbidity with other affective disorders, alcohol or substance abuse, dissociative disorders, and some of the anxiety-based personality disorders (e.g., obsessive-compulsive) is well established, especially in military populations. Detecting or differentiating the precise or focal PTSD symptoms from the usual larger array of psychiatric symptoms is a major challenge in relatively brief social media communications.

Developing a lexical ontology for a medical condition begins with the root term itself (PTSD) and any synonyms, hypernyms, or hyponyms. The canon of focal symptoms must then be organized into more experience-near categories and several possible categorizations must be reviewed. In the ontology developed for this project, it was determined that five common language groupings, Behavioral, Cognitive, Emotional, Functional and Physical, would constitute Instance Level 1 (presented in Table 2.2). The actual terms to be used in the narrative text search are 65 focal symptoms (Instance Level 2 presented in Table 2.2). These represent expert opinion consensus on the actual language used by patients and their families to describe the symptoms and problems in clinical interviews. Some of these terms are common language transliterations of technical neuropsychiatric symptoms (e.g., *flashbacks* and *spells* for the actual symptom of re-experiencing) while some are the common language consequences of having PTSD, such as acquired behavioral or interpersonal deficits (e.g., impaired activities of daily living (ADLs) such as losing the ability or confidence to drive a vehicle). These terms form the basis for actual text analyses, whether by trained clinicians or using search software. Table 2.2 presents the Instance Level 1 groupings and the Instance Level 2 term counts.

The final list of 65 ontological terms to be used by expert evaluators to assess or annotate the social medium narratives of military veterans includes an array of observable behaviors, subjective experiences of the unique symptoms of PTSD (e.g., flashbacks), as well as the negative symptoms of the disorder (e.g., interpersonal avoidance). Some of these search terms are unique to PTSD and some are more generalized symptoms or behaviors found among patients with chronic neuropsychiatric disorders.

The development of a lexical ontology to detect PTSD *signals* from social media narrative text follows the standard psychometric test development steps. First, the sample terms are developed using negotiated expert opinions. Secondly, the intra-rater and the inter-evaluator reliabilities need to be examined to refine the text annotation process. Finally, once the coding guidelines have been established, the various types of validity are inferred using standard correlational analyses. The next step is to determine the operating characteristics of the model, for example, determining which subset of ontology terms is most useful in identifying either clinical group membership or the probability of PTSD for an individual (e.g., *somewhat likely*) based exclusively on the narrative text.

The emerging information processing discipline of network science holds considerable promise for developing validated software screening tools for the early detection of high-risk behaviors or psychiatric syndromes in vulnerable populations known to avoid professional attention. The prevalence and incidence of undiagnosed PTSD among post-deployment military populations makes this type of endeavor especially timely and important.

References

1. American Psychiatric Association (1980) Diagnostic and statistical manual of mental disorders, 3rd edn. Author, Washington, DC
2. American Psychiatric Association (2000) Diagnostic and statistical manual of mental disorders (4th edn. Text Revision). Author, Washington, DC
3. Schwarz ED, Kowalski JM (1991) Malignant memories: PTSD in children and adults after a school shooting. J Am Acad Child Adolesc Psychiatry 30:936–944. doi:10.1097/00004583-199111000-00011
4. Pentland A (2008) Honest signals: how they shape our world. The MIT Press, Cambridge, MA
5. Frank LK (1939) Projective methods for the study of personality. J Psychol 8:343–389
6. Rossini ED, Moretti RJ (1997) Thematic Apperception Test (TAT) interpretation: practice recommendations from a survey of clinical psychology doctoral programs accredited by the American Psychological Association. Prof Psychol Res Pract 28:393–398
7. Murray HA (1943) Thematic Apperception Test: manual. Harvard University Press, Cambridge, MA
8. Morgan CD, Murray HA (1935) A method for investigating fantasies: the Thematic Apperception Test. Arch Neurol Psychiatry 34:289–306
9. Luhrmann TM (2000) Of two minds: the growing disorder in American psychiatry. Knopf, New York
10. Blake DD, Weathers FW, Nagy LM, Kaloupek D, Klauminzer G, Charney DS, Keane TM, Buckley TC (2000) Clinician-administered PTSD scale (CAPS) instruction manual. National Center for PTSD, Boston, MA

Chapter 3
Data Sources

Abstract Any project relying on data analysis is only as good as the data sources selected. The data sources used for the Community for Education, Wellness and Support (CEWS) project were carefully selected from the ever-increasing options of forums, blogs and social networks to ensure that the set contained relevant data sources to be used for training data. Following the selection of the data sources, tools were developed to extract the maximum value from the data. The Psychological Information Library (PIL), containing references to the most up to date collection of resources and texts concerning PTSD was also used to tune the analytics engine. Relevant blogs and forums have been identified by the team's experts, brought into common environment and cleaned to enhance the accuracy of the analytics results. Open-ended questions from the Brain Fitness questionnaires provide a unique way to collect PTSD-specific textual input from the users.

3.1 Introduction

Probably the single most important step in performing any type of data analysis is the selection of data sources. The growth of Internet usage, specifically the explosion of social networking websites, has resulted in unbounded growth of unstructured data volumes that are available on any given subject. For human analysts, sifting through large volumes of data related to the task at hand is time-consuming and can cause delays and fatigue which in turn cause deterioration of the analyst's performance and accuracy.

Automated solutions for data analysis address the issue of volume; however, they bring to light a different set of issues. While significant advancements have been made in computer program capabilities, when it comes to determining relevance, they still are not as accurate as humans, and thus function best when fed a *curated* stream of documents that have been pre-screened using some type of human approval process. The more sophisticated the analytical algorithm, the more sensitive it is to the data format, thus requiring pre-processing cleanup steps. For CEWS, the data sources selected fell in the following categories:

- Psychological Information Library (PIL)
- Brain Fitness Free-Text Questions
- Forums

For the purpose of the project, only relevant forums were selected as data sources during the process of curating information. In an effort to provide better control over the data obtained during the testing phase, data from some sources, i.e., microblogging services such as Twitter was excluded. Data from these sources were deemed unnecessary since the CEWS testing environment specifications did not include building a closed microblogging service, and, due to Twitter's unique formatting conventions, posts frequently do not directly contain discussions of psychological symptoms; instead posts related to PTSD on Twitter often contain links to blogs and forums where such discussions take place.

3.1.1   Psychological Information Library (PIL)

The Psychological Information Library (PIL), a selection of texts and resources available in print, online, or in both formats, includes reference texts (books and journal articles), online assessment tools, clinical information, and links to relevant social networking resources. The materials contained in the PIL pursue several objectives:

- Provide guidance and *best practice* recommendations to psychological professionals and users of CEWS
- Provide centralized access to information on methods of counseling
- Provide clinicians with up-to-date information on methods and modes of diagnosis and treatment
- Allow individuals with PTSD and their family members to gain access to information on symptoms, treatments, and methods of coping with the condition

While there are countless publications and websites addressing various aspects of PTSD, the quality and information vary widely. Some resources present incomplete information, while others are essentially a collection of links without guidance on their intended use. The PIL presently hosts approximately 300 references of currently available resources. Each has been identified through a review and evaluation process and then vetted by psychologists participating in the project to ensure all materials selected are high quality and representative of the studies, resources, and tools available.

Table 3.1 Open-ended questions in the NeoCORTA self-assessment

1	Please describe any changes you've noticed in your physical, functional, or sensory abilities since deployment.
2	Since returning from your deployment, how have your lifestyle, habits, and behavior changed?
3	Over the last few months, how would you describe your thinking abilities (memory, concentration, problem solving, etc.)? How do your current abilities compare to your pre-deployment abilities?
4	Over the last few months, how would you describe your emotional well-being? How do your current emotional patterns/reactions compare to your pre-deployment patterns/reactions?
5	Please describe any other changes, problems, or unusual experiences you've had since deployment.

The forums and blogs for inclusion are highly ranked compared to other similar websites.[1] Books, peer-reviewed articles, and recent research studies were identified for inclusion based on input from the participating psychologists, and a review of the most-current and most frequently cited literature. Additional articles from government agencies and consumer news sources have also been included in the PIL database to ensure that the knowledge base includes clinical information and resources, as well as materials for a lay audience.

In addition, a subset of 18 items from the reference material contained in PIL was manually selected and processed for inclusion in the SentiGrade™ infrastructure. This satisfied two needs: (1) the identification of additional terms for inclusion in the PTSD ontology, and (2) the identification of co-occurring word patterns used in questionnaires and clinical literature on PTSD. The selection of resources included in this subset was based on input from the participating psychologists, with additional selection criteria of the resources being available gratis and without requiring that users log in to access them.

3.1.2 Brain Fitness Free Text Questions

NeoCORTA[2] has developed a set of five *free text* questions that are included as part of the anonymous self-assessment questionnaires (see Table 3.1). All text from these fields is automatically sent to the SentiGrade™ engine, and the qualitative

---

[1] "Ranking" according to Alexa (http://www.alexa.com). Alexa is one of several providers of free, global web metric. Others include Google Analytics, ComScore and Quantcast. Alexa uses a toolbar to measure website statistics. Once installed, the toolbar collects data on browsing behavior which is transmitted to Alexa's website where it is stored and analyzed. Other data sources beyond the toolbar are taken into account, i.e. domain name age, number of indexed pages in search engines, etc.

[2] NeoCORTA (http://www.neocorta.com) is a company in the brain health, fitness and wellness space. Its product, the Brain Fitness Toolkit (BFT), is a self-administered survey producing individual reports containing recommendations and interventions for maintaining and improving brain health. The BFT has been adapted for the purposes of this project to incorporate the PCL-M (PTSD

results (sentiment/signal scores) of the processing are returned to the NeoCORTA system to be processed alongside the user's answers to the Brain Fitness multiple-choice questions.

CEWS envisioned a comparative study of the scores calculated via the automatic text analysis and the results of the Brain Fitness questionnaire-based evaluations.

3.1.3   Social Media—Blogs and Forums

In much the same way that reference materials in the PIL have been curated and represent the most applicable materials, social media sources have been used as data sources for the project with an eye toward their relevance and frequency of updates. The selection criterion for the data sources is of great importance, as these sources are intended for use in an automated analysis system. Obtaining a curated set of text samples from these resources eliminates *noise* sources that do not contain information pertinent to PTSD discussions. Additionally, the elimination of materials that are not updated frequently ensures that materials gathered are current, and that processing resources were not wasted on materials that would not add substantive value. The selected sources fall into two categories:

- External sources identified by as being relevant. A subset of data from these sources was used to train the automated analytics system, and the results reported here are based on the data from these external sources.
- Internal sources which use the social network environment developed for the project. Anonymous test users were given access to the environment and the resulting data were used to validate the accuracy of the automated solutions.

A suite of data collection and pre-processing tools was developed to provide real-time automated submission of anonymous social media data to SentiGrade™ and to facilitate access to that data for both curators and participating clinicians. The data collection suite has been built using a collection of open source tools, including the PHP programming language, the LINUX operating system, a relational database, and cURL libraries.[3] The core of the suite is a crawler engine that seeks out and collects data from relevant websites identified as possible sources of material.

The external data source websites (see Table 3.2) identified fed into the data collection system and processed. For each data source, the information architecture was studied and then configured in the crawling engine. The crawling engine searched the sources and stored the data into a staging area on a relational database.

The staging area tries to preserve the data in the original format by retaining the original content and topology of the data. Data in the staging area is manually

---

CheckList—Military Version) and five PTSD-related free text questions so that its analysis engine can screen for signals of PTSD.

[3] cURL (http://curl.haxx.se/) is a command line tool for transferring data with URL syntax.

Table 3.2 Data sources and document count

Source	Document count
http://www.militaryonesource.com/	6,090
http://forums.militaryspot.com/	52,852
http://www.notalone.com/	1,138
http://forum.avbi.org/	468
http://combat.ptsdforum.org/	5,846
http://www.politicalforum.com/	86,349
http://www.politicalfray.com/	17,456
http://www.militarysos.com/forum/	1,955,509
http://www.militarytimes.com/forum/	254,024
http://www.depressionforums.org/forums/	411,494
http://www.soberrecovery.com/forums/	1,268,072

spot-checked for validity and value for the task at hand. Once determined to be appropriate for the purposes of the project, data is cleaned in preparation for submission to the classifier-training environment, which is used, among other things, for generation of the Human Annotated corpus described in a later section.

The cleaning step involves removal of non-ASCII characters and stripping off most HTML tags and JavaScript, while retaining the topology and decorations of the source data as much as possible. These include:

1. The topology of the posts: the parent child relationship between posts (essentially any thread structure of the post)
2. The time stamp of the post
3. Any other decoration or other tag associated with the post

After the data is loaded into the classifier training environment it is displayed and organized into a structure that is as similar to the source structure as possible. This allows a human annotator to browse and explore the data in a natural format. The annotator may also query the corpus using free text queries.

As soon as a document is selected for inclusion in the classifier training set, it can be annotated (scored) using the scoring tool shown in Fig. 3.1. The original document is followed by classification options, which the annotator selects and associates with the document. The annotator, usually a psychologist, can make two classifications, one based on the clinical evaluation of the document text and the other solely based on the text of the document. The annotator can also score the signals identified in the text. These signals correspond to the top-level of the ontology and are:

- Behavioral
- Cognitive
- Emotional
- Functional
- Physical

I've noticed a much more sensitive sense of smell. Before, nothing bothered me as far as smells go. Now, if someone in the office is wearing certain perfumes it can cause headaches, nausea, and stress. I've had a lot of issues with one of my student workers. They feel offended when I tell them they can't wear that perfume to work anymore. Get over it! Can't stand people crowding me or leaning against me. Work clothes make me feel restricted, but that is because I have to dress up. I find I forget a lot. Got in the car one day and had trouble remembering which side of the road I'm supposed to be on. Oh well, I'm sure there is more. I certainly can't stand loud crowds. Church semi-okay. A seat in the back helps and the only real stress is the beginning and end. Local baseball team's game? Not a chance.

☐ No Symptoms

					RSCR
PTSD					
- CLINICAL:	◎ Likely	◎ Somewhat Likely	◎ Not Likely	◎ DK	2
- TEXT:	◎ Likely	◎ Somewhat Likely	◎ Not Likely	◎ DK	2.5
- COGNITIVE:	◎ Frequently	◎ Sometimes	◎ Rarely	◎ Never	4
- EMOTIONAL:	◎ Frequently	◎ Sometimes	◎ Rarely	◎ Never	3
- BEHAVIORAL:	◎ Frequently	◎ Sometimes	◎ Rarely	◎ Never	1
- PHYSICAL:	◎ Frequently	◎ Sometimes	◎ Rarely	◎ Never	2
- FUNCTIONAL:	◎ Frequently	◎ Sometimes	◎ Rarely	◎ Never	2.5

Fig. 3.1 TIDO (Text In-Data Out) document annotation screen

The corresponding score for each selection is also displayed, for information purposes.

When an adequate sample of training documents has been generated, the system runs an export of the training data in the form of a comma separated values (CSV) file and submits it to the classification engine. Salient fields in the exported training data are:

1. A document ID that uniquely identifies the text of the training exemplars.
2. A cleaned text of the document, which includes ASCII characters, stripped of HTML and other markup.
3. An annotator-ID that uniquely identifies the annotator.
4. A set of classifications and signals along with the corresponding scores selected by the annotator.

Regardless of the data source, resulting textual documents are submitted to the SentiGrade™ engine via the SentiMetrix© API. Each source category has a unique identifying code, which allows for sorting of the results by source category. There are also facilities enabling clinicians and other authorized users to sort and track data by the anonymous user ID and perform analysis over time. Note that CEWS users are assigned anonymous user IDs, so no personal identifying information (PII) is ever collected or entered into CEWS, thus ensuring anonymity and confidentiality. The only people who can identify CEWS users are the clinicians who recruited the users and assigned them the anonymous user IDs. The clinicians hold appointments with the VA and are bound by HIPAA regulations and their professional code of ethics not to release any user PII to anyone associated with the project. Furthermore, all user PII is stored at secure VA facilities.

Chapter 4
Text Analytics

Abstract The exponential growth in the use of social media and creation of unstructured data has elevated the importance of text analysis technologies. From political campaigns to business intelligence and national security, the need for the automated extraction of information from unstructured textual data has led to the development of a number of specialized approaches to address the unique needs of particular markets. This project takes a unique approach, which applies text analysis techniques to detection of psychological signals that may be symptomatic of Post-Traumatic Stress Disorder (PTSD). While standard text analysis technologies have been used, this particular project required heavy customization of the toolset. The Text-in, Data-out (TIDO) tool, built to facilitate the human annotation of the training corpus, has been used to capture the human psychologists' knowledge and make it available to the analytical engine for training.

4.1 Introduction

Text analytics: a discipline combining tools, techniques, and methods used to extract structured information from unstructured (presumably textual) data, has been around for over half a century. In 1958, writing in the *IBM Systems Journal*, H.P. Luhn described a system for automatic profiling of textual documents that would "…utilize data-processing machines for auto-abstracting and auto-encoding of documents and for creating interest profiles for each of the 'action points' in an organization. Both incoming and internally generated documents are automatically abstracted, characterized by a word pattern, and sent automatically to appropriate action points." The article was titled "A Business Intelligence System" [1], but as computerized management systems entered the mainstream in the last quarter of the twentieth century, there was a shift from business intelligence (BI) systems, which focused primarily on structured (fielded) numerical data in the 1980s, for the obvious reason that such data was easier to analyze.

V. Kagan et al., *Sentiment Analysis for PTSD Signals*, SpringerBriefs in Computer Science, DOI 10.1007/978-1-4614-3097-1_4, © The Author(s) 2013

Toward the 1990s two trends converged as the *old* BI model became commoditized, spurring the need for new analytical techniques. Concurrently, one of the side effects of the explosive popularity of the Internet in the last 20 years has been the exponential growth in volume of textual (unstructured) data that is available. In addition to billions of "traditional" web pages[1] and hundreds of billions of emails sent daily, there are now over 150 million blogs online, as based on reports from 2011 by BlogPulse.[2] Over 750 million individuals worldwide use Facebook and there are over 150 million Twitter users, all of whom send trillions of messages, contributing to the ever-growing corpus of textual data. If this data is combined with internal corporate document stores, data due to the recent popularity of *e-governments* worldwide, and data from the effects of the increasingly powerful mobile devices including mobile phones, tablets, and tablet computers, the numbers become truly difficult to comprehend.

The Internet has been called a *universal echo chamber*, and it has been said that the answers to many questions wait in cyberspace for those who know how to ask the question. Making sense of the massive supply of data available can be difficult, however. Humans are simply not fast enough to collectively cope with the current level of information overload, let alone make reasonable use of the data available. This brings automated text analytics back to the forefront of academic, governmental, and commercial research; and based on recent successes, the use of text analytics, also known as text mining, has grown to encompass many more areas. Collecting and analyzing textual data from blogs, forums, and chat rooms allows consumer products companies to find out how successful their new offerings are compared to their competitors. Politicians use social media analytics to quickly gauge their constituents' reaction to the latest campaign statements. Twitter streams are used to predict the stock price movements.

While the term *text mining* has traditionally been associated with internal enterprise applications, text analytics is now providing actionable insights to many segments of the business, government and political activities. Early text mining solutions considered a text source to be a *bag of words*. Techniques were developed to account for word variants such as abbreviations, plurals, and other stems, as well as multiword patterns (n-grams.) Analysis involved counting frequencies of words and terms and classifying documents by topic. However, these early systems lacked an ability to understand the semantics—the meaning—contained within a given document.

As technological means and the science behind them developed, advanced text analytics started to offer the capability to extract vast amounts of actionable information from the body of an unstructured text. Going beyond feature extraction (names, places, dates), text analytics software can now detect relationships, evaluate *voice of the customer*, and extract other actionable information, for example identifying most/least favorite features of a product. Modern text analytics systems make use of techniques like clustering, classification, and link analysis. An area of

---

[1] Google claimed to have processed one trillion unique URLs, as reported by Information Week on July 25, 2008.

[2] BlogPulse was a search engine and analytic system for blogs, which is currently owned by NM Incite, a joint venture between Nielsen and McKinsey.

particular interest is predictive modeling, especially in areas such as risk analysis, fraud detection, and national security. Textual sources are inherently feature-rich and multidimensional, making text analytics a natural area for application of statistical techniques. Machine-learning algorithms and deep linguistic analysis allow a large degree of semantic *understanding* of the text.

4.2 Application to a Particular Field: Psychology/PTSD

Many of the text analysis techniques available today can be applied to diverse subject areas like marketing, politics, and medicine. In order to obtain the best possible results, a certain degree of domain-subject knowledge is required.

The first preparatory step involved is data collection or the identification of a corpus—a set of textual materials, available on the Web or stored in a database, a content management system, or a file system—for analysis. Selection of appropriate data sources for the subject of interest is extremely important to producing meaningful results. For example, blogs, which discuss football, are unlikely to generate meaningful insights into national security issues.

Named entity recognition is another area that requires careful planning. Named entity recognition is the use of gazetteers or statistical techniques to identify named text features: people, organizations, place names, stock ticker symbols, and certain abbreviations. The use of contextual clues may be required to decide where, for instance, *Ford* refers to a former U.S. president, a vehicle manufacturer, a movie star, or some other entity. Both the entities themselves and the context require certain degree of pre-existing domain knowledge. A common method of providing a text analytics system with domain knowledge is via ontologies, structured frameworks that combine shared vocabulary with the definition of objects and/or concepts, and their properties and relations.

At the same time, recognition of features such as telephone numbers, email addresses, or quantities (with or without units) can be discerned via regular expressions or other pattern matching constructs without specific domain knowledge. For example, in the sentence *Regardless of the topic, you can contact Ford by calling (111)-222-3344 or by writing to aaa@ford.zzz* it does not matter if the text mentions President Gerald Ford, Ford the car maker or actor Harrison Ford—the contact information can be identified and extracted the same way in any case. Co-reference—the identification of noun phrases or other terms that refers to the same object—is also not domain-specific in most cases. Consider, for example the sentence *We really like XXX; its YYY is ZZZ* In this sentence, without understanding what XXX, YYY or ZZZ are, it is clear that *its* references XXX.

One of the areas of text analytics that has received attention in recent months is sentiment analysis [2–4]. Sentiment analysis involves discerning subjective (as opposed to factual) material and extracting various forms of attitudinal information: sentiment, opinion, mood, and emotion. Text analytics techniques are helpful in analyzing sentiment at the entity, concept, or topic level and in distinguishing between opinion holder and opinion object. This approach is increasing in popularity, and is being utilized by corporations seeking to extract quantified opinions regarding their products and services from the overabundant posts on Twitter, Facebook, and blogs.

As the sentiment analysis engines grow in popularity and capabilities, novel applications for the technology are being explored. For this research project the SentiGrade™ sentiment analysis engine has been modified to detect the frequency and intensity of the specific PTSD-related experiences described in blogs, forum posts, and free-text portions of traditional surveys. The modifications to the commercial off-the-shelf (COTS) available SentiGrade™ system are described in chapters five and six, while the approach and preparatory steps taken to build domain-specific knowledge is outlined below.

4.3   PTSD Data

The collection of PTSD-related data represents two distinct corpora: (1) clinical documentation describing all aspects of the psycho-physiological disorder, and (2) forum discussions authored by individuals suffering from the disorder or their friends and family. These two small corpora are the main sources of term sets that enable manual and automated classification of future related resources.

The manual classification task involves hand-crafting a taxonomy, a hierarchical classification schema specifying parent-child relationships, such as *is a kind of* or *is a subtype of*, that serves as a knowledge-management platform. This platform describes the classes, term-sets, and relations of all the concepts included in the main topic. For example, psychological disorders exhibit certain common attributes—Symptoms, Treatments, and Causes—but may differ in what the values for those attributes are. Thus, it is important to be able to differentiate between disorders in order to reduce or eliminate false positive or false negative classifications. The *relations* in the taxonomy are often quite simple and amount to merely *containment* relations—also known as *IS-A* relations. That is, words in the simplest sorts of hierarchies are connected by specificity—*poodle IS A dog, dog IS A mammal*. More complex hierarchies may involve relations such as *part-whole* such as *wheel IS-PART_OF_A car*. The hierarchies associated with physical and emotional disorders (medical taxonomies in general) often contain many different relation types [5].[3] More general relations used in medical taxonomies are simply association-type hierarchies (symptom x *IS_ASSOCIATED_WITH* disorder y) and may contain what are called *pertainyms*—words, which merely pertain to certain concepts. In the taxonomy created for PTSD, no particular relations were specified, although these relations can be specified if needed at a later time, once the structure is in place. Encoding specific relations in hierarchies beyond the simplest type is

---

[3] See http://www.artechhouse.com/GetBlob.aspx?strName=ananiadou_984_samplech03.pdf for more information on medical taxonomies.

Table 4.1 A sample of PTSD taxonomy hierarchy

PTSD			
Symptoms			
	Behavioral		
		Avoids Activity	
		Recklessness	
	Cognitive		
		Flashbacks	
		Memory Loss	
	Emotional		
		Anger	
		Fears	
	Functional		
		Cannot Work	
		Does Not Socialize	
	Physical		
		Attacks	
		Nightmares	

used mainly for creating expert systems, which is not necessary for the purposes of document classification.

In creating the taxonomy, human analysts need to review clinical material to determine how to group the correct term-sets under the correct headings. The first task is to gather lists of *symptom-type* words, *treatment-type* words, and the like to figure out where key differences are found that separate the greater concepts. This task provides the base understanding, which can enable follow-on automated processes. Such automated processes may come in the form of document classification—automatically separating large corpora for example into *documents about depression* vs. *documents about PTSD*—expanding the taxonomy terms automatically [6], and automatically translating documents to find similar documents in other languages. An example of taxonomy entries for PTSD symptoms is provided in the Table 4.1.

4.4   Procedures and Methods in Data Analysis

Following the creation of manually defined taxonomies, one of the first tasks is automated Topic detection. While human analysis can be useful for the initial knowledge base, identifying all the different themes and topics within a corpus is best accomplished by statistical natural language processing methods. Several views of the Topic profile of documents are created following data aggregation. Topic profiling is a separate task from classification. Frequently an entire collection of documents can be run together, knowing that their topic blends may be complex. (See references [7–9] for the most frequently cited research on Latent

Dirichlet allocation (LDA) for topic modeling) The corpus can be divided as desired but it is always wise to run the entire corpus as a whole at least once to inform divisions later.

When Topic models are run for the project, the algorithm (the LDA algorithm) looks for word densities and contexts to find the words that are most *interesting*, meaning the most likely to be good topic indicators. The number of topics selected per document corpus is free to vary and often is dependent on the use of the output. That is, there may be a use for a *coarse* output where there are few topics chosen and each word in the selection can apply over many of the topics. Alternatively, it may be more useful to learn about all the topics that are possible and getting a very subtle output.

Once the best number of topics is selected, other dimensions can be analyzed. For example, it is often interesting to run a bigram (multi-word-phrase) report to identify the *interesting* phrases in the corpus. Because phrases are lower in frequency than unigrams, this data tends to yield productive results when trying to craft rule-based solutions for classification. Multi-word topical units are often very specific and precise indicators of a topic.

Although each topic in the selection (regardless of the number) is nameless, a good knowledge of the corpus will make it obvious what the Topic collections represent. The set of topics is a good way to judge potentially how many classes may be involved in classification. For example, often sub-topics emerge very strongly and suggest a multi-class approach rather than a binary approach to a task. It is helpful to learn which words contribute the most to which topics to gain an understanding of *how important* the *interesting* words are to sub-topics. For example, if a COUNT file is generated, the frequency and count of words across topics can be obtained, thereby providing a sense of the depth and breadth of lexical coverage. Generally, words corresponding to the *main* topic (in this case PTSD) will be very broad and appear in many of the topics whereas sub-topics like words representing *treatments* will be more concentrated in a few topics.

4.5   Performance and Best Practices

Understanding the densities and coverage properties of topic words is helpful when approaching the classification task for two reasons. First, if a rule-based classifier is desired, the understanding of specific lexical indicators derived from the topics and how strongly they connect to topics can inform which lexical items can be used in rules and whether those rules would perform better on recall or precision. Second, if statistical approach is desired, the topics can be transformed into weightings to make the classifiers more accurate.

Thus the process involves these steps to ultimately create an accurate classification system when faced with a new data set:

- Experiment with topic profiles, find best number
- Find topics for the whole corpus, then corpus divisions

- Find unigram and bi-gram topic sets
- Find the lexical coverage for the topics
- Decide how best to use the topics to help the classification model

Ultimately, classifier testing must be conducted in rounds with various blends of training and testing data to optimize results. Training data is part of the overall data set used to help statistical models understand the underlying word profiles of documents. Often part of the corpus is *held out* in order to subsequently test the model to see how well it understands the class distinctions. Not every blend of training and test data will be the same, and different quantities of each also produce different results. For example a common training-testing split is 90:10. The *new* data out in the world that eventually is fed into the model is the ultimate determination of accuracy. Poor performance does not always improve with additional data if the classes are poorly understood from the beginning. However, well-understood data sets can be fairly small but perform well if the procedures outlined here are followed.

Successive rounds of performance testing are followed by changes in the classification algorithms chosen, as well as different training and testing sample trials. When an acceptable level of accuracy is achieved, the classifier is saved and used as an object in a user-facing application. The levels of *acceptability* are dependent on the fault tolerance of the ultimate end user.

It is worth noting that, even in an inherently difficult field as detection of psychological signals, a custom-tuned software systems may perform remarkably well. While not all topics were detected with equal efficiency (perhaps due to the fact that some were not present in the source documents), the overall accuracy of the system in deciding the likelihood of PTSD approached that of the human experts (see Chap. 7).

4.6   Human Annotation

Understanding text is inherently a human activity. Software systems, and especially sentiment analysis engines, aspiring to derive in-depth semantic insight into textual documents, often make use of human-annotated (HA) data sets for initial training. An HA corpus generated by subject matter experts provides the engine with domain-specific knowledge, serving as the foundation for tuning and weighting of the linguistic and statistical models used to *understand* text. Human experts function as *off-line teachers*, so the better the quality of the HA corpus, the better the results.

There are many HA data sets available, covering various domains in different languages and targeting many applications. To better serve the purposes of this research project, a custom HA set was built, utilizing the expertise of clinical psychologists and making use of the data collected. For that purpose, a document annotation tool called Text-in, Data-Out (TIDO) was developed to guide and simplify the annotation process. TIDO allows navigation to a particular forum or topic, as well as access to posts, comments, and/or replies (Fig. 4.1).

Each post that is determined to contain any of the *signals* outlined below is scored on seven PTSD-related attributes.

Text In - Data Out (TIDO)

Forums   Search

	Forum
❱	✉ Avbi Forum
❱ My account	✉ Combat PTSD
❱ Log out	✉ Depression Forums
	✉ Military One Source
	✉ Military SOS
	✉ Military Spot
	✉ Not Alone
	✉ Training-GeneralMilitary
	✉ Training-PTSD
	✉ Training-RelatedForums
	✉ Training-Sports-Politics Forums
	✉ Training-TBI

Fig. 4.1 Forum data collected and available for annotation

PTSD-related signals:
- Frequency/Intensity of Symptoms (grouped as Cognitive, Behavioral, Emotional, Functional, and Physical)

  - Frequently
  - Sometimes
  - Infrequently
  - Rarely
  - Never

- No Symptoms, Select this box if the post displays no symptoms of PTSD (Fig. 4.2)

4.6.1 Likelihood of PTSD Syndrome

- Clinical: Rating based on the clinician's background knowledge. Rating options include:

  - Likely
  - Somewhat Likely

I've noticed a much more sensitive sense of smell. Before, nothing bothered me as far as smells go. Now, if someone in the office is wearing certain perfumes it can cause headaches, nausea, and stress. I've had a lot of issues with one of my student workers. They feel offended when I tell them they can't wear that perfume to work anymore. Get over it! Can't stand people crowding me or leaning against me. Work clothes make me feel restricted, but that is because I have to dress up. I find I forget a lot. Got in the car one day and had trouble remembering which side of the road I'm supposed to be on. Oh well, I'm sure there is more. I certainly can't stand loud crowds. Church semi-okay. A seat in the back helps and the only real stress is the beginning and end. Local baseball team's game? Not a chance.

☐ No Symptoms

PTSD					RSCR
- CLINICAL:	○ Likely	○ Somewhat Likely	○ Not Likely	○ DK	2
- TEXT:	○ Likely	○ Somewhat Likely	○ Not Likely	○ DK	2.5
- COGNITIVE:	○ Frequently	○ Sometimes	○ Rarely	○ Never	4
- EMOTIONAL:	○ Frequently	○ Sometimes	○ Rarely	○ Never	3
- BEHAVIORAL:	○ Frequently	○ Sometimes	○ Rarely	○ Never	1
- PHYSICAL:	○ Frequently	○ Sometimes	○ Rarely	○ Never	2
- FUNCTIONAL:	○ Frequently	○ Sometimes	○ Rarely	○ Never	2.5

Fig. 4.2 Interface displaying a document and scoring options

- Not Likely
- DK (Don't Know)
- Text: Rating based on signals within the document text. Rating options include:
- Likely
- Somewhat Likely
- Not Likely—text does not contain any signals
- DK (Don't Know)—text shows no indications

The *Clinical* rating allows a clinician to *infer* the likelihood of the syndrome using their clinical training and experience, whereas the *text* rating is scored using the *words* in the post. For example, if a clinician can infer from reading the post that the user has incurred a traumatic brain injury (TBI) but does not have PTSD, then the Likelihood of Syndrome-Clinical will be low for PTSD—whereas the Likelihood of the Syndrome based on the actual words and phrases used in the post may be scored high for PTSD.

4.6.2 Frequency/Intensity of Symptoms

The user may place the mouse over a term to hover and view a few brief, related terms. These terms do not include the entire list of related terms for the syndrome, but do serve as a reminder of what is meant by each *symptom*. Rating options related to frequency/intensity of symptoms include (Fig. 4.3):

- Frequently
- Sometimes
- Rarely
- Never

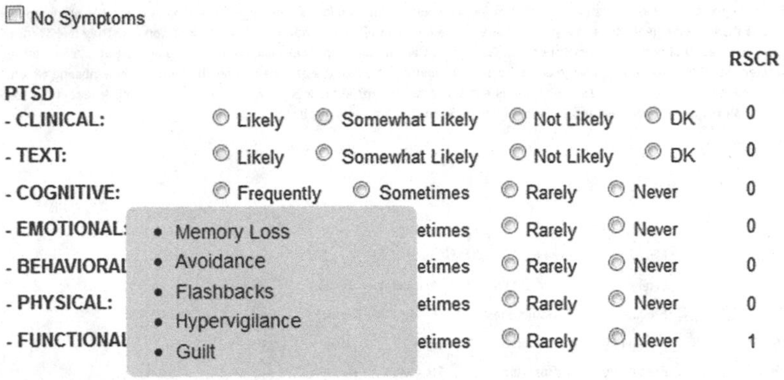

☐ No Symptoms

RSCR

PTSD
- **CLINICAL:**   ◎ Likely   ◎ Somewhat Likely   ◎ Not Likely   ◎ DK   0
- **TEXT:**   ◎ Likely   ◎ Somewhat Likely   ◎ Not Likely   ◎ DK   0
- **COGNITIVE:**   ◎ Frequently   ◎ Sometimes   ◎ Rarely   ◎ Never   0
- **EMOTIONAL:**   • Memory Loss   etimes   ◎ Rarely   ◎ Never   0
- **BEHAVIORAL**   • Avoidance   etimes   ◎ Rarely   ◎ Never   0
- **PHYSICAL:**   • Flashbacks   etimes   ◎ Rarely   ◎ Never   0
                   • Hypervigilance
- **FUNCTIONAL**   • Guilt   etimes   ◎ Rarely   ◎ Never   1

Fig. 4.3 TIDO scoring options with overlay information

4.7   Human Annotation Results

The result of the HA process is a data set containing both the text of the original document and the associated annotation metadata. The HA data sets are transmitted from the annotation tool to the text analysis system to be used for training of SentiGrade™, and for comparison with the machine-generated results. A document along with the HA is shown in the following table and the description of the process and analysis leading to the results follows (Table 4.2).

The analysis process of the document in the above table follows the steps:

1. Perform a first pass by reading the document to get an overview of the content
2. Use the annotator's clinical expertise to determine whether PTSD is a viable diagnostic hypothesis based on the document content
3. Review and classify the text for ontology-related terms or symptoms suggesting PTSD
4. Rate the frequency of each of the five PTSD symptoms
5. Validate the text classification following the rating of the frequencies of the reported or inferred symptoms

During the analysis the following questions are posed and analyzed:

1. Are there clinical indicators of PTSD?
   In the text no catastrophic event was mentioned or implied, just some changes in perception, affective reactions to situations, and comfort level with people. This would not indicate PTSD, but rather some type of hypersensitivity issue involving Axis II personality traits (e.g., paranoia, schizoid, schizotypal). Then, the memory problems are unusual and are more suggestive of TBI. The statement about remembering which side of the road to drive is very odd unless the person was stationed in a left-driving country. Finally, the principle symptom is changes in olfactory sensitivity, which is more medical-neurological than psychiatric. Therefore, the PTSD evaluation is *Not Likely,* even though very mild analogs of some of the defining PTSD symptoms (Hypervigilence/Arousal/Avoidance) are voiced. No re-experiencing was mentioned.

Table 4.2 A human annotated document as produced through TIDO

Field	Content
Document-ID	Node-197613
Type	Forum
Source Name	Training-PTSD
Source Author	Admin
Title	I've noticed a much more sensitive sense of smell.
Body	I've noticed a much more sensitive sense of smell. Before, nothing bothered me as far as smells go. Now, if someone in the office is wearing certain perfumes it can cause headaches, nausea, and stress. I've had a lot of issues with one of my student workers. They feel offended when I tell them they can't wear that perfume to work anymore. Get over it! Can't stand people crowding me or leaning against me. Work clothes make me feel restricted, but that is because I have to dress up. I find I forget a lot. Got in the car one day and had trouble remembering which side of the road I'm supposed to be on. Oh well, I'm sure there is more. I certainly can't stand loud crowds. Church semi-okay. A seat in the back helps and the only real stress is the beginning and end. Local baseball team's game? Not a chance.
ptsd_CLINICAL	Not Likely
ptsd_TEXT	Not Likely
ptsd_COGNITIVE	Frequently
ptsd_EMOTIONAL	Sometimes
ptsd_BEHAVIORAL	Never
ptsd_PHYSICAL	Never

2. Are there text indications of PTSD?

   Some sub-clinical symptoms broadly compatible with the DSM-IV-TR criteria are cited, but none reach the significant threshold needed to assign a PTSD likelihood. The key omission is, again, re-experiencing of a trauma.

3. Are there symptoms reported that fit the ontology terms?

   Cognitive symptoms are rated *Frequent,* notably the memory problems, hypervigilence, distractibility by loud, active situations, and proximity to other people; also the stress reported seems more cognitive than affective (crabby/irritable).

   Emotional symptoms are rated *Sometimes.* Ongoing, episodic, state-specific symptoms are reported and always in work or social-group situations (There is no mention of home life). None are common anxiety or common dysphoria, rather cognitive-affective (stress) and affective discomfort in crowd situations.

   The nausea and headaches are Physical symptoms, but these are situation-specific to some scents only, thus the rate of *Never.*

   There is no information regarding Behavioral symptoms, thus they are rated as *Never.*

   Clearly, the consistency and accuracy of the HA process plays an important role in the subsequent performance of the software classifier trained on the HA set. As mentioned in Chap. 7, human experts do not always agree in their assessment of text documents with respect to the presence of the psychological signals.

References

1. Luhn HP (1958) A business intelligence system, IBM Journal of Research and Development, Volume 2 Issue 4, October 1958, Pages 314–319
2. Cesarano C, Dorr B, Picariello A, Reforgiato D, Sagoff A, Subrahmanian VS (2006) OASYS: an opinion analysis system. Proceedings of AAAI-2006 spring symposium on computational approach to analyzing weblogs
3. Sleator D, Temperley D (1991) Parsing English with a link grammar. Carnegie Mellon University Computer Science technical report, CMU-CS-91-196
4. Subrahmanian VS, Reforgiato D (2008) AVA: adjective-verb-adverb combinations for sentiment analysis. Intell Syst 23(4)
5. Ananiadou S, McNaught J (eds) (2006) Text mining for biology and biomedicine. Artech House, Boston, MA, pp 43–66
6. Richardson M et al (2010) Using SAS® Text Miner 4.1 to create a term list for patients with PTSD within the VA. SESUG 2010: The Proceedings of the SouthEast SAS Users Group, Savannah, Georgia
7. Blei D et al (2003) Latent Dirichlet allocation. J Mach Learn Res 3:993–1022
8. Blei DM, Lafferty JD (2006) Correlated topic models. In: Weiss Y, Schölkopf B, Platt J (eds) Advances in neural information processing systems 18. MIT Press, Cambridge, MA
9. Wei X, Bruce Croft W (2006) LDA-based document models for ad-hoc retrieval. Proceedings of the 29th annual international ACM SIGIR conference on research and development in information retrieval, 6–11 August 2006, Seattle, WA

Chapter 5
Scoring Engine

Abstract The rapid growth in the use of social media has given rise to several new types of text analytics, such as buzz monitoring, opinion mining, and Sentiment Analysis (SA). SentiMetrix©, Inc., a company specializing in Sentiment Analysis, has built a scalable modular SentiGrade™ engine that provides near-real-time analysis and precise granular sentiment scores for textual documents across a variety of domains. SentiGrade™, combining several open-source components with proprietary technology developed by the SentiMetrix© team, utilizes in-depth analysis of the grammatical structure of each sentence and applies human-trained models to quantify the sentiment towards multiple topics. The engine was expanded to incorporate new TAPIR algorithms to better accommodate the needs of the psychology-related subject and the project.

5.1 Introduction

The rapid growth in the use of social media (sometimes also known as Consumer-Generated Media, or CGM) has given rise to several new types of text analytics, such as buzz monitoring, opinion mining, and Sentiment Analysis (SA). While the terms are often used interchangeably, and a significant overlap exists between the respective technologies and results, there are noticeable differences between the three areas.

- **Buzz monitoring** focuses primarily on frequency and volume of mentions of a particular topic. This information is particularly useful when analyzing the outcomes of marketing campaigns. It allows quick detection of the topics that have caught the attention of the Internet users; identification of the websites, blogs and twitted discussions that focus on topics of interest; and is often used to determine the influencers— people, and sources whose opinions on certain subjects seem to shape the corresponding public interest. When polarity (positive/negative, or positive/neutral/negative) and authority (how credible a particular source is with regard to the given subject) are added to raw buzz data, the results and the technologies used bring buzz monitoring closer to opinion mining or sentiment analysis.

V. Kagan et al., *Sentiment Analysis for PTSD Signals*, SpringerBriefs in Computer Science,   33
DOI 10.1007/978-1-4614-3097-1_5, © The Author(s) 2013

- **Opinion mining**, as the name implies, concentrates on opinions—thought-out conclusions that are, nevertheless, still open for discussion. Opinions are often classified into subclasses, for example: *views* are usually more subjective; *beliefs* imply conscious acceptance; *convictions* are strongly held beliefs; and *persuasions* typically indicate beliefs that are based on assurance of their truth.
- **Sentiment analysis** in its pure form does not attempt to judge objectivity or the strength of the factual base, but rather measures the intensity and polarity of the *feelings* expressed towards the topic of interest. Because of that, it is best suited for measurement of emotions expressed in the textual documents.

  - There are several approaches to calculating sentiment analysis scores, each with its strengths and weaknesses. They differ in the models used—from purely statistical to pure natural language processing (NLP)-based to hybrids—as well as in the sensitivity (calculating overall sentiment of entire documents versus calculating sentiment toward particular topic), and granularity (ranging from simple positive/negative to large, potentially infinite, number of levels between extremely negative and extremely positive). Such differences manifest themselves externally not only in the results produced, but also in the resources required for calculations and in speed of processing. Most of the commercially available systems make one sort of tradeoff or another, making them better suitable for a particular market segment.

5.2   SentiGrade™

SentiGrade™, the sentiment analysis engine powering the SentiMetrix© offerings, has its roots in the OASYS system [1] developed at the University of Maryland at College Park. SentiMetrix© acquired the exclusive commercialization rights to the OASYS technology in 2006 and has significantly improved and expanded the reach and accuracy of the original algorithms, while building it into a commercial-grade high-performance sentiment analysis system.

SentiGrade™ aims to achieve the optimal blend of precision, granularity and speed of processing by combining NLP techniques for in-depth analysis of text with statistical methods used to tune the scoring model. Implemented on top of a modular architecture, SentiGrade™ can be scaled to achieve very high performance while preserving the precision and granularity of the resulting scores.

5.3   SentiGrade™ Architecture

SentiGrade™ consists of three distinct sub-systems, each with well-defined functionalities:

1. **Data Gathering/Input Subsystem**. The role of this subsystem is the gathering and accepting of external data, performing initial cleanup and making data available to the core scoring engine.

2. **Core Scoring Engine**. This is the *brain* of the system, where most of the analytical tasks are performed. As the documents are processed, they either are rejected (when no sentiment is detected) or result in a set of scores and associated metadata that are made available to the front end.

3. **Front End**. The results generated by the core engine are stored in the front-end database that has been optimized to minimize response times for incoming queries. The SentiGrade™ dashboard (shown in Fig. 5.3) and a set of customizable report-generating scripts extract and format the data from the front-end database for a variety of presentation possibilities.

The SentiMetrix© Application Programming Interface (API) provides a way to submit data to the engine for processing, and to retrieve the resulting scores.

The SentiGrade™ system works in a pipeline fashion. Each module can be run on a separate machine. The task of each module is to prepare the data for the next module. Each module waits for the tasks of the previous module(s). A module can start executing once the preceding module sets a database table flag. The output of each module is to write something into the database—as a consequence, communication between the sub-systems and sub-system components is accomplished via a relational database.

5.3.1   Architecture Diagram

The logical architecture of the SentiGrade™ system consists of several modules shown in Fig. 5.1 below. Each module may consist of several sub-modules, some of which will be discussed later in the document.

5.3.2   Functional Architecture

In this section, the various modules of the SentiGrade™ system are briefly described.

5.3.2.1   Input Modules

The function of any input module is to insert incoming documents into the processing queue. Currently the system supports three types of input modules:

- Crawlers return the contents of the pages selected either from a pre-configured set or from results of a Google search for a particular query
- Spinn3r client receives data from the Spinn3r service. Spinn3r provides a *fire hose* data feed that includes updates from over 10,000 news sites, over 14 million blogs, Facebook, and Twitter
- API-based input, allowing clients to create their own data submission applications external to SentiMetrix©

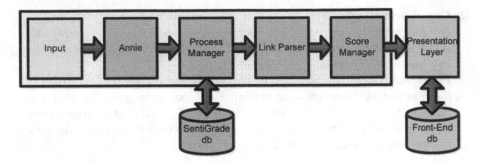

Fig. 5.1 Architecture of the SentiGrade™ system

It is worth noting that neither crawling nor the Spinn3r feed were utilized to acquire data for the project. All the data came from the CEWS sources, providing a uniform approach to data acquisition and privacy concerns.

5.3.2.2   Annie Module

For a document in the input queue, the Annie Module extracts the document (if remote), translates it (if needed) by invoking a third party translation service, breaks it into sentences and identifies entities and entity types. The Annie module also performs pronoun resolution. If no sentences or no entities are detected, the document is excluded from further processing.

5.3.2.3   Process Manager Module

For each sentence of each document the Process Manager Module identifies opinion-expressing words (OEWs) including adverbs, verbs, and adjectives and their corresponding raw (uncombined) scores. The scores will later be combined in the Link Parser Module using the link structure of the sentence. Sentences that do not contain any OEWs are eliminated from further processing.

5.3.2.4   Link Parser Module

For each sentence, the Link Parser builds a link grammar, tying OEWs with entities within the same sentence. The module makes use of the link grammar parser developed at the Carnegie Mellon University [2].[1] The Link Parser constructs a marked-up tree, similar to the one in Fig. 5.2 below, identifying the relationships that are then used by scoring modules.

---

[1] More information on the link parser available at http://www.link.cs.cmu.edu/link/.

Fig. 5.2 Sample Link Parser
marked-up tree

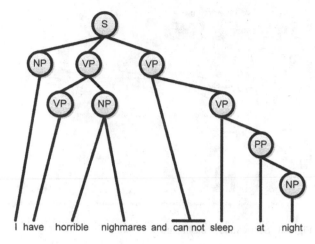

5.3.2.5 Score Manager Module

The Score Manager Module first calculates a combined score for each sentence-topic pair. It then aggregates the sentence-topic scores into a single document-topic score by averaging the scores of the sentence-topic pairs involving the topic.

5.3.2.6 Front End Modules

The SentiGrade™ dashboard allows registered clients to run arbitrary queries against the last 12 months of data from the public SentiMetrix© data set, generating sentiment trend and volume charts. Results for up to five terms can be compared.

In addition to standard Boolean AND and OR operators, a context string can be entered as part of the query. Context strings are used to narrow down the domain of the query by only considering the documents containing the string. For example, the query *Obama* will return every document where opinion toward the entity "Obama" was detected, while *Obama + President − Michelle* will only consider documents where Obama is mentioned as president while Michelle Obama is not mentioned at all.

The dashboard provides certain syndication capabilities. The charts can be published to Facebook and Twitter, and the charts graphics can be saved on the user's computer (Fig. 5.3).

5.3.2.7 SentiGrade™ Databases (Back End and Front End)

The backend database serves as the main pipeline queue for processing of the incoming documents. Each processing module reads the next document to be processed from the backend database, and writes back the results. The front-end database has been optimized for speedy retrieval of results in response to user queries.

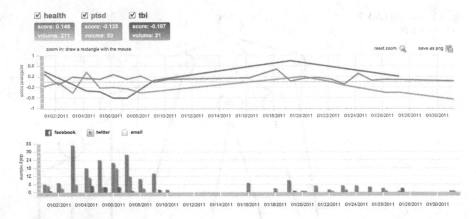

Fig. 5.3 SentiGrade™ dashboard

All the dashboard queries go against this database. It contains scoring results, grouped by month, in a de-normalized form. The indices for the last 12 months are in-memory, minimizing access to the disks.

5.3.3   Physical Architecture

All SentiGrade™ components run on Amazon EC2 virtual servers under Fedora 8. Using EC2 cloud allows fast scale-up (or down) in response to the prevailing processing needs. The modular architecture of SentiGrade™ allows running of multiple processing pipelines on a shared set of servers, as well as running dedicated and/ or customized processing partially on dedicated and partially on shared servers.

5.4   SentiMetrix© API

The SentiMetrix© API is a RESTful[2] layer that allows authorized parties to submit data for processing to SentiGrade™ engine and to retrieve the results. It supports uploads of single documents as well as batch processing, and allows clients to specify terms of interest, overriding the default *calculate sentiment for all entities* model. Administrative tools to authorize clients, generate client ID keys, and monitor processing status are available.

The API has been modified to accommodate the needs of CEWS. New data fields have been added to the protocol to allow submission of anonymous user IDs, and to retrieve results rolled up according to the PTSD Ontology described later in this section.

---

[2] Representational State Transfer (REST) is a style of software architecture for distributed hyper-media systems. A RESTful web service is a simple web service implemented using HTTP and the principles of REST. (http://en.wikipedia.org/wiki/Representational_state_transfer).

5.4.1 Architecture

The API is a standalone application running within a Tomcat instance. It is composed of three layers: presentation, services and persistence. The presentation layer uses the services to generate the XML response. The service layer represents the business logic. Finally, the persistence layer is responsible for interacting with the database and file system.

5.4.2 API Architecture Diagram (Fig. 5.4)

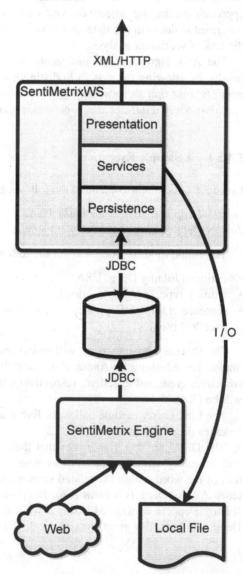

Fig. 5.4 SentiMetrix© API architecture

5.4.3   Opinion Expressing Constructs

The algorithms at the core of the SentiGrade™ system make use of the Scored Word
Bank, a database of < word, score > pairs that allows SentiGrade™ to be easily
trained for working with text from specific domains. During processing, the scores
for OEWs or their synonyms detected in the documents are combined to produce
the final score for the topics they relate to.

The original OASYS system relied on the Scored Word Bank consisting primarily of adjectives, with the scores learned from several hundred of news articles [1].

Keeping up with the sentiment analysis research [3–5], SentiMetrix© has significantly improved on that approach, by introducing a unified sentiment-scoring
approach combining adjectives, verbs and adverbs (AVA). The AVA algorithm,
described in detail in [6], extends the verb classification ideas of Beth Levine [7] to
the task of sentiment analysis.

The AVA algorithm has noticeably increased the accuracy of SentiGrade™
results, by allowing the system to distinguish between sentences like *concert was
good, he said that the concert was good, he mentioned that the concert was good*
and *he strongly reiterated that the concert was good*.

5.4.3.1   A Sample Execution

Consider a document containing the following text:

Johnny Depp is a great actor in the USA.
Johnny Depp made several excellent movies.

The Annie module would extract the following information:

- entities:{Johnny Depp, USA},
- entities_type:{person, location},
- sentences:{Johnny Depp is a great actor in USA.$#$ Johnny Depp made several
  excellent movies}.

The Process Manager, then, will process each sentence making use of the information passed along by Annie. Assuming that 0.7 and 0.9 are the values for the
adjectives great and excellent, respectively, the result of processing the sentences
will be (Table 5.1).

The Link Parser module builds the link grammar trees and assigns the following
linkages (Figs. 5.5 and 5.6; Table 5.2).

The OEW_arr flag T indicates that the opinion expressing word is associated
with the entity while F means it is not associated. The oew_position counts the position of the word within the related sentence where that entity is found. In the sentence *Johnny Depp is a great actor* the position of the OEW (great) is 4 because
Johnny Depp is considered a single word (entity). The parser associated Johnny
Depp with the OEW great, but did not do the same for USA.

Table 5.1 Results of processing sentences through Annie and Process Manager

SentenceID	Entities	Ent_type	Oew_val	Oew_type
1	Johnny Depp, USA	Person, location	0.7	Adjective
2	Johnny Depp	Person	0.9	Adjective

Fig. 5.5 Link grammar tree
and mark-up for SentenceID 1

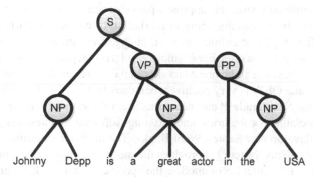

Fig. 5.6 Link grammar tree
and mark-up for SentenceID 2

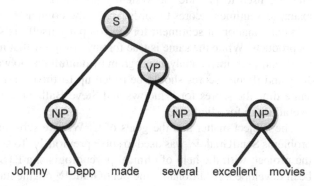

Table 5.2 Link Parser linkages for SentenceID 2

SentenceID	Entity	Oew_position	Oew_arr
1	Johnny Depp	4	T
1	USA	4	F
2	Johnny Depp	4	T

The Scoring module would use the Process Manager and Link Parser information to associate OEWs with the entity "Johnny Depp", combine the corresponding values and come up with the resulting sentiment score. There are several models for combining the scores, from simple average to more elaborate that take into account the overall tone of the document. In this (admittedly simple) example, the best approach would be to average the sentence-level score, resulting in the sentiment score of 0.8 for the entity *Johnny Depp*.

5.5 Modifications Needed for the PTSD Domain

The questions the SentiGrade™ engine was developed to answer originally generally fall in the category *given the set of data sources D and topic T, how does the sentiment S(T) expressed in the documents comprising D change over time*. As outlined above, this approach provides actionable information in many areas, ranging from manufacturing to marketing to national security to political campaigns. The topics or entities involved change from area to area, as do the OEWs and the associated scores. For example, *loud* has a negative connotation when viewed in the context of engine noise and should therefore result in negative sentiment score. The same OEW is very positive when used to describe, for example, a fire alarm. While the SentiGrade™ engine returns accurate scores for a variety of segments using its default vocabularies and existing software, sometimes it proved necessary to develop new Scored Word Banks. The methods described in OASYS: An Opinion Analysis System [1] provides the mechanism for such improvements.

To further accommodate the specifics of particular segments, dedicated ontologies are used to provide the system with the particular domain knowledge. For example, sentiment scores towards Apple (the computer company) may be thought of a combination of sentiment for the company itself, its stock, its executives, and its products. While the same is true for any company that manufactures any kind of products, a sentiment analysis program by default has no way of knowing that Steve Jobs and iPhone scores should be rolled up to the overall Apple score, but at the same time the scores for Windows and Steve Ballmer are to be rolled up into the overall score for Microsoft.

The subject matter and the goals of CEWS are substantially different from the problems SentiGrade™ was used to solve previously. To accommodate the needs of the project, with the help of clinical psychologists, a PTSD-specific ontology has been developed. Additionally, the SentiGrade™ engine has been used as the foundation for the system for performing text analysis for PTSD in real-time (TAPIR) The API was also modified to provide additional functionality required for CEWS, and a brand-new dashboard was built.

5.5.1 Ontology

SentiGrade™ system had no prior knowledge of medical terminology, nor did it understand how to categorize the colloquial terms people use to describe medical or psychological symptoms and match them to symptoms of PTSD. The system did, however, have a capability to integrate domain-specific ontologies, specifically designed to address such situations. The materials available through the Psychological Information Library (PIL) and a large number of external Internet sources have been examined, and sample data has been collected. Selected PIL materials and sample data were subjected to computer analysis, to identify prevailing topics, word frequency, and word clustering patterns. NeoCORTA, the company behind Brain Fitness questionnaires, provided the initial list of symptom categories.

The resulting ontology combines scientific terminology and colloquial terms in a two-level structure. At the top level (Instance Level I) there are five manifestation type signals, covering all the recognized symptoms of PTSD:

- Behavioral
- Cognitive
- Emotional
- Functional
- Physical

This common five-signal structure was used for the CEWS environment. It determined the format of the SentiGrade™/TAPIR results, defined the granularity of the dashboard charts, and integrated into the Human Annotation tool.

The next level of the ontology (Instance Level II) presented the symptoms characteristic for the corresponding top-level signals. This level included both the professional terms learned from the psychological materials and clinical psychologists on the team, as well as colloquial terms detected in the sample documents. For example, the Emotional signal includes the following symptoms:

- Emotional
  - Irritability
  - Exaggerated emotional reactions
  - Craziness
  - Anger
  - Shame
  - Numbed
  - Negative mood
  - No pleasure
  - Restricted emotions
  - Pissed off
  - On edge
  - Phobia
  - Fears
  - Numbing

The Instance Level II terms form the basis of the text patterns that the SentiGrade™/TAPIR engine used for generation of the signal and syndrome scores for each processed document.

5.5.2   TAPIR

While using many of the same components and the same data flow as the standard SentiGrade™ engine, the architecture of the PTSD-specific version can be viewed as consisting of four main components:

- **TAPIR Word Categories.** The first component of the TAPIR architecture consists of an extensive list of PTSD-related terms, extending the PTSD Ontology and divided up into categories (e.g., *anger* might be a category containing a list of words referencing anger). The categories are further mapped onto the PTSD ontology Instance Level I signals.
- **TAPIR PTSD Analysis Tool.** The TAPIR PTSD Analysis Tool performs the following task.

    - **Input:** It receives a blog post as input.
    - **Output:** For each category C above, the TAPIR PTSD Analysis tool assigns a score to the category. Thus, the result returned by the TAPIR PTSD Analysis tool is a set of (category, score) pairs reflecting the score for the given input blog on each of the various categories.

- **TAPIR Final Score Tool.** The set $\{(C_1, S_1), ..., (C_n, S_n)\}$ of scores returned in the previous step for each category is combined to generate the scores for each of the five signals defined in the PTSD Ontology. These scores, in turn, are combined into a single integrated score reflecting the overall probability that an individual reference in the input blog post B is indicative of PTSD. There are many ways in which the final score from TAPIR can be defined. Multiple alternative scoring methods will be explored and evaluated on a validation data set via a standard *k-fold cross validation* study to evaluate the different scoring methods. The best scoring method will then be incorporated into the final TAPIR software.
- **The TAPIR Classifier.** This component takes the final score generated by the preceding component and classifies the subject of any blog post into one of four categories:

    - Likely to indicate PTSD
    - Somewhat likely to indicate PTSD
    - Not likely to indicate PTSD
    - Can't tell

5.5.2.1   TAPIR Word Categories

Using the PTSD Ontology as the foundation, a suite of words was developed describing the symptoms defined in the Ontology. In addition, for each word in this word list, a *polarity* was assigned. The polarity of a word refers to whether the sentence indicates if the symptom described by the word occurs or does not occur.

For instance, *sleep* is a word stem associated with insomnia. A sentence that says *I always enjoy a great night's sleep* indicates a positive occurrence of the word *sleep* and does not indicate insomnia. On the other hand, insomnia is indicated by a negative occurrence of the word *sleep*. For instance, in the sentence *I was unable to sleep*, the word sleep is *negated* through the word *unable*.

Table 5.3 A sample word list representation

Category	Word stem	Polarity	Score
Anger	Anger	Positive	0.5
Anger	Temper	Positive	0.6
Insomnia	Sleep	Negative	0.4
Stress	Stress	Positive	0.5
Stress	Calm	Negative	0.5

The word lists used describe whether a word must occur positively or negatively in a sentence for the symptom described by the word to be deemed to occur. For example, *sleep* must occur negatively for insomnia to be indicated, not positively.

Each of our word lists will therefore be represented as a table with the schema (*Category, Word Stem, Polarity, Score*) where *Score* is the score of the word on a 0–1 scale—0 indicates no occurrence of the symptom, while 1 indicates a complete occurrence of the symptom. A small sample portion of such a table is shown below (Table 5.3).

The first row of this table says that when the word *anger* occurs positively in a sentence, then it has a score of 0.5 as far as the category *anger* is concerned. Likewise, the third row says that if the word stem *sleep* occurs in a sentence, then the category *insomnia* occurs with a score of 0.4—thus, a positive occurrence of *sleep* will not cause any score to be assigned to the *insomnia* category. It must occur negatively.

5.5.2.2 TAPIR PTSD Analysis Tool

The goal of the TAPIR PTSD Analysis tool is to take a blog post B and a category C (from the above list of 19 categories) and assign a probability score between 0 and 1 for the intensity of symptoms in category C associated with blog post B.

A score of 0 means (according to TAPIR) there is a 0 % probability that a subject referenced in blog post B has the symptoms associated with category C. A score of 1 means (according to TAPIR) there is a 100 % probability that a subject referenced in blog post B has PTSD.

To see why the TAPIR PTSD Analysis Tool works, a couple of simple examples drawn from real blog posts identified as representative data samples must be examined (Fig. 5.7).

Blog post B1 given above is a real blog post, replete with both spelling and grammatical errors. Let us consider three categories:

- **The anger category**. We see that the phrase "… always angry short tempered …" occurs in this blog post. TAPIR searches for words in the *anger* category that appear (in stemmed form) in the above blog post. In the above article, the word stems "anger" (from "angry") and "short temper" (from "short tempered") appear in the word list associated with "angry". Moreover, the polarity of the occurrences of these words is positive (i.e., the sentence does not negate them).

> **BLOG POST B1:** I'm recently married to an incredible Iraq combat veteran
> since I've known him the only thing we have dealt with ptsd related is his
> inability to get a honest hood night normal sleep... Until recently it's all
> falling apart, he's always angry short tempered doesn't remember things
> and idk what's going on! He wants to have children and thinks things are
> fine and he's slowly decreasing in happiness and liveliness I feel like he's
> falling back into major PTSD symptoms how do you deal with your spouse
> with PTSD??

Fig. 5.7 Blog post B1

SentiGrade™'s proprietary word list assigns a score to the word "angry" (or
rather to its stem, "anger") and to the word "short temper". Suppose these scores
are 0.5 and 0.6, respectively, indicating that the strength of these words implies a
degree of belief that a subject being described in blog post B is angry with a probability 0.6 (take the maximum of the two scores).

- **The insomnia category.** If the *insomnia* category (similarly stemmed) is also
  considered, it can be seen that the words "inability to get an honest hood night
  normal sleep" appear in this blog post—presumably the "hood" in this sentence
  is misspelled and should have been "good". The inference of correct spellings of
  misspelled words was beyond the scope of this effort. In this sentence "honest
  hood night sleep" references the word "sleep" which is associated with insomnia
  when negated. The word *inability* that precedes sleep in this sentence negates the
  occurrence of the word sleep. The negated form of sleep may have a score of 0.4,
  for instance, denoting a 40 % probability that this article references lack of sleep
  in the subject being discussed. The existing SentiMetrix© scoring technology
  was used for this purpose.
- **The memory loss category.** In the same vein, we see the phrase *doesn't remember* in the blog post, indicating a lack of memory. The word stem *remember* is
  negated and as a consequence, may have a score of 0.3.

Thus, in the case of blog post B1, the PTSD Analysis Tool returns the set of pairs
{(anger, 0.6), (insomnia, 0.4), (memory loss, 0.3)}. None of the other 19 categories
are referenced in this post and hence, their score (for blog post B1) is implicitly 0.

Let us consider the second blog post B2 below, also taken from the set (Fig. 5.8).

Consider blog post B2 above (items in red are highlighted by the annotator of
this document, not by the blogger). Consider the categories *depression* and
insomnia.

- **The insomnia category.** The subject of blog post B2 is sleep-walking. Suppose
  the PTSD word category table has the tuple (insomnia, sleep walk, positive, 0.3)
  in it, denoting that positive occurrences of words with the stem "sleep walk"
  imply that the blogger's subject has PTSD with strength 0.3. In this case, we see
  that the pair (insomnia, 0.3) should be in the answer returned by the PTSD Word
  Analysis Tool.

> **BLOG POST B2:** My fiance has been home 11 months. He was deployed to Afghanistan. He has <u>depression</u> and PTSD and he is seeking help for that. However, he <u>sleep walks</u> every night to the point where he endangers himself. I had to move back into my parents house because it got so bad. He acts out his dreams no matter what they are and this has ONLY since he has been home from deployment. He has never had problems with this before. The VA Hospital doctors say it is his PTSD but they can't get him to a sleep clinic for 18 more months. We don't have health insurance and cannot afford it at this time. My parents still cover me and the VA is all my fiance has.   I was wondering if anyone else has experienced this and if so what did you do?

Fig. 5.8 Blog post B2

- **The depression category.** Suppose the PTSD Word Category Table has the tuple (depression, depress, positive, 0.5) in it, denoting that positive occurrences of the word stem "depress" imply that the blogger's subject has PTSD with strength 0.5. In this case, the pair (depression, 0.5) should be in the answer returned by the PTSD Word Analysis Tool.

Thus, in the case of this document, the PTSD Word Analysis Tool returns the set {(insomnia, 0.3), (depression, 0.5)}. The blog post B2 contains no evidence of any other kind of PTSD category that the subject of the blogger is suffering from.

To implement the PTSD Word Analysis Tool, a score for each word in the word list must be found.

1. Search for occurrences of a given word stem (e.g., anger) in a document
2. Identify if the occurrence of the word is positive or negative—this can be done using standard algorithms such as in [1]
3. Examine the PTSD Word Category Table and determine if there is a tuple of the form (category, word, polarity, score) where the polarity and word coincide with the word being sought and the polarity in the table coincides with the polarity of the occurrence of the word in the sentence

   (a) If yes, insert the pair (word, score) from the table into the tentative answer list ANS

4. If the answer list is non-empty, choose the max value of the scores in the answer list ANS and return (word, max score) back to the user

These four steps are repeated for each word in the word list.

5.5.2.3   TAPIR Final Score Tool

The scores discussed above may be viewed as a function χ that maps each PTSD category to a score. For instance, χ(depression) is the value of the category "depression" (applied to a specific blog post, of course) in a given arbitrary, but fixed blog

Table 5.4 Mapping functions and their definitions

Function name	Definition	Comments
Min	$\mu_{min}(c) = min\{\mu(c) \mid c$ is any category$\}$	Score is the smallest score assigned to any category
Max	$\mu_{max}(c) = max\{\mu(c) \mid c$ is any category$\}$	Score is the biggest score assigned to any category
Avg	$\mu_{avg}(c) = avg\{\mu(c) \mid c$ is any category$\}$	
Weighted mean	$\mu_{wt\text{-}avg}(c) = \Sigma_{category\ c}\ w_c * \mu(c)$ /number of categories	Computes the weighted mean of scores assigned to each category where w_c is the weight assigned to category c

post B. Likewise, χ(insomnia) is the value of the category *insomnia* as derived by the PTSD Word Analysis Tool for a given blog post B.

The goal of the TAPIR Final Score Tool is to merge all these scores into a single, unified score. μ is used here to denote this *merging* function which takes a single function χ as input, and returns as output, a number in the [0, 1] interval denoting the overall probability that the subject of a given blog post B has PTSD.

There are many ways in which μ can be defined. However, whichever method is used to define μ, it appears clear that μ should be a monotonic function. What this means is that if the two blog posts B1 and B2 are considered, and χ applied to B1 always returns a smaller score, in every category, than it does for B2—in this case, the final score given by μ to B2 should be higher than the score given to B1. This makes sense because *on every dimension* (i.e. *category*), the indication that B2 has PTSD is higher (or equal) than B1—so the final score should respect this.

Formally, suppose two scoring functions—χ_1, χ_2,—are considered and returned by the PTSD word analysis tool on certain inputs (not necessarily the same). Then $\chi_1 \leq \chi_2$, if and only if for every category c, it is the case that $\chi_1(c) \leq \chi_2(c)$.

The final scoring function μ is *monotonic* if and only if whenever $\chi_1 \leq \chi_2$, it is the case that $\mu(\chi_1) \leq \mu(\chi_2)$. There are many examples of monotonic scoring functions, some of which are given in the table below (Table 5.4).

It is clear that each of these functions is monotonic, as long as the weights are all greater than or equal to zero in the last case. However, further experimentation will be needed to determine which method works the best.

Using a similar approach, the scores for individual categories will be combined into scores for the Instance Level I signals defined in the PTSD Ontology.

5.5.2.4   TAPIR PTSD Classifier

Once the preceding module generates the TAPIR Final Score, for a particular blog post, there is a need to classify the subject of the blog post with respect to the likelihood of the subject of the post having or not having PTSD. This is accomplished by training the system on the Human Annotated (HA) corpus of sample data.

First, a table was built and populated with the values from the HA data set. Each row in this table corresponded to a single blog post. The columns included columns for each of the signals and two columns specifying whether the person has PTSD or no as marked by the human annotators—the first column was the clinical decision on whether they are likely or not to have PTSD, while the second column indicated whether the annotator thinks the text of the blog indicates PTSD is likely or no. A classification algorithm was used to learn a classifier that characterizes the relationship between the columns corresponding to the signals and these two dependent variables. This classifier, once trained on training datasets, was later applied to validation and evaluation data to assess its accuracy.

References

1. Cesarano C, Dorr B, Picariello A, Reforgiato D, Sagoff A, Subrahmanian VS (2006) OASYS: an opinion analysis system. Proceedings of AAAI-2006 spring symposium on computational approach to analyzing weblogs
2. Daniel Sleator and Davy Temperley (1991) Parsing English with a link grammar. Carnegie Mellon University Computer Science technical report, CMU-CS-91-196
3. Benamara F et al (2007) Sentiment analysis: adverbs and adjectives are better than adverbs alone. Proceedings of the 2007 international conference on weblogs and social media (ICWSM07). www.icwsm.org/papers3--Benamara-Cesarano-Picariello-Reforgiato-Subrahmanian.pdf
4. Turney P (2002) Thumbs up or thumbs down? Semantic orientation applied to unsupervised classification of reviews. Proceedings of the 40th annual meeting association for computational linguistics (ACL 02), pp 417–424
5. Kim SO, Hovy E (2004) Determining the sentiment of opinions. Proceedings of the 20th international conference on computational linguistics (COLING04), ACM Press, pp 1367–1373
6. Subrahmanian VS, Reforgiato D (2008) AVA: adjective-verb-adverb combinations for sentiment analysis. Intell Syst 23(4)
7. Levin B (1993) English verb classes and alternations: a preliminary investigation. University of Chicago Press, Chicago

Chapter 6
System Overview

Abstract In this section we describe the overall architecture of the system built for the project. It diagrams the general data flow, illustrating how the anonymous test users and evaluators are able to use the system to submit text documents for analysis and view and evaluate the results. The hardware specifications for the servers used to run the text analysis system is outlined. The chapter also covers the modifications made to the SentiGrade™ engine and provides a detailed description of the changes made to the standard SentiMetrix©, Inc. web services application program interface (API) to support the project's needs. A detailed description of the SentiMetrix© project-specific dashboard is provided, outlining the rationale behind the visualization approach chosen, and explaining the drill-down capabilities made available to the evaluators.

6.1 Overall Architecture

The system designed for the research project allows for the collection of anonymous user input from a pre-defined set of sources (Brain Fitness surveys, forums, blogs, chats, and comments, of which only Brain Fitness surveys, forums and comments were used) and generation of assessments geared toward the detection of likelihood of PTSD-related signals (Fig. 6.1).

The system generates a variety of anonymous reports, viewable via the Brain Fitness reporting dashboard and the SentiMetrix© dashboard. The Brain Fitness dashboard incorporates the results of text analysis performed by the SentiMetrix© sentiment analysis engine, and the SentiMetrix© dashboard presents results extracted from all anonymous user-submitted textual data.

The evaluators use the dashboards to compare the results of the automated processing by Brain Fitness and SentiMetrix©. The results of the evaluation will be instrumental in assessing the achievement of the overarching goal of the

V. Kagan et al., *Sentiment Analysis for PTSD Signals*, SpringerBriefs in Computer Science,   51
DOI 10.1007/978-1-4614-3097-1_6, © The Author(s) 2013

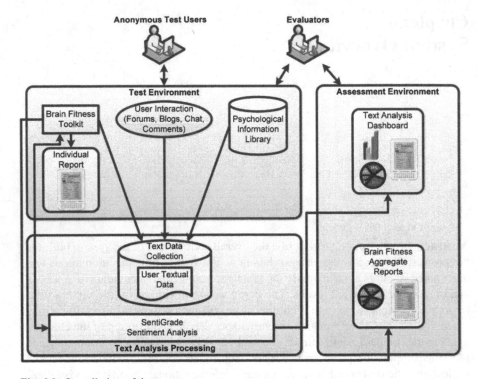

Fig. 6.1 Overall view of the system

project—building an automated system for reliable large-scale real-time detection of relevant psychological signals.

While it is important to understand the overall system design approach and goals, this chapter focuses primarily on the text analysis system. The changes made to the commercially available SentiMetrix© sentiment analysis product will be described, as will the data flow within the system and the dashboard used to display the results of text analysis.

6.2 SentiGrade™ Environment

SentiMetrix© has built its modular engine to run in a virtual computing cloud (currently, the Amazon EC2 service is used). Cloud-based hosting allows easy scaling to accommodate virtually any load, ensuring efficient use of computing resources. It also allows creation of isolated clusters for projects requiring customization of the engine. To achieve near-real-time results for the complicated text processing involved in detection of the psychological signals, the project-specific SentiMetrix© cluster consists of three servers (Fig. 6.2).

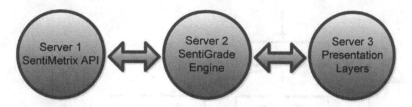

Fig. 6.2 SentiMetrix© server layout

Server	EC2 model	Specifications
1	Micro Instance	2 EC2 Compute Units 613 MB RAM 1 TB EBS Disk
2	Extra Large Instance	13 EC2 Compute Units 34.2 GB RAM 850 GB Instance Storage 2 TB EBS RAID
3	Small Instance	1 EC2 Compute Unit 160 GB Instance Storage 500 GB EBS Disk

Table 6.1 SentiMetrix© server specifications on Amazon EC2

All SentiGrade™ components run on Amazon EC2 virtual servers under Fedora 8. The server environment configurations are outlined in Table 6.1.

6.3   SentiMetrix© API

The SentiMetrix© application program interface (API) was modified to accommodate the formats of the data sources and reporting requirements of the project. In particular, several meta-information elements were added to the API to allow easier back tracing of individual documents submitted via the Brain Fitness questionnaires. In addition, the results retrieval API has been updated to provide the means for optionally requesting results for individual signal scores, top-level syndrome scores for PTSD, or both.

6.3.1   API Technologies Used

The persistence layer uses Java Persistence API (JPA) with Hibernate as the persistence provider when interacting with the database. The presentation layer uses Spring3 for the Model View Controller (MVC) framework. All the layers are wired together using the Spring framework.

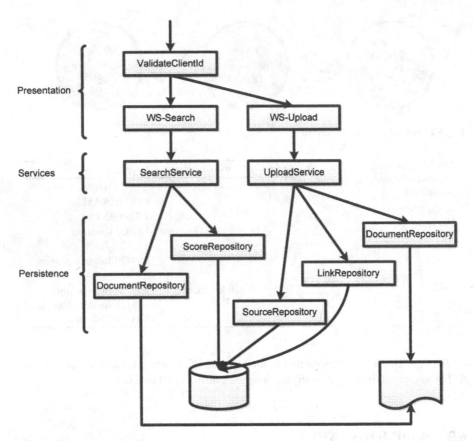

Fig. 6.3 SentiMetrix© API architecture

6.3.2   Design

There are five repositories:

- One to interact with the SentiGrade™ engine input queue
- One to interact with the *sources* table
- One to interact with the file system to create input files
- One to interact with scores data
- One to interact with document data

  The service layer presents two services:

- One to search for scores and documents
- One to handle uploads and to check on the processing of an uploaded batch

  The presentation layer has two controllers that will respond to the four types of requests and one filter to validate client IDs (Fig. 6.3).

6.3.3   API Interfaces

The SentiMetrix© APIs are REST web services, which allow submission (*upload*) of documents for processing, either one by one or in batches, monitoring and retrieval of results for each upload, searching for results in a particular subset of documents (as defined by query parameters such as date range, source, and language), and retrieval of headlines and content (via URL) of processed documents.

6.3.3.1   Upload Documents

This service is used to push data to SentiMetrix© for analysis. Data is placed into a queue for processing and the results of the analysis are made available at a later time.

To submit documents for processing a POST request is submitted to a URL having the following format: http://www.myhost.com/api/rest/upload.

Multiple documents can appear in a POST.

The API is expecting the request body to be of content-type = application/x-www-form-urlencoded. This is to make initiating the request from the browser easy with HTML or JavaScript (JS).

Request Parameters:

None

Form Fields:

clientKey (mandatory)

   string representing anonymous user; assigned by SentiMetrix©

term (optional)

   batch specific terms for which sentiments will be extracted; no other terms will
      be extracted

title (optional)

   title of document

url (optional)

   URL to fetch the document. If URL is used the content argument will be ignored

content (optional)

   text to analyze

published (optional)

   date when this document was originally published. Format is yyyy-MM-dd'T'HH:mm:ss.SSSZ. Example is 2011-06-13T22:56:32.895-0400.

externalRef (optional)

> identifier attached to document used by external systems. This value is passed through to results so that external systems can tie the results to the original document.

profileId (optional)

> identifier attached to document used by the SentiMetrix© system to group documents.

Return Codes:

200—Success
400—invalid input
403—the account specified is invalid
404—the resource does not exist
500—the server encountered an internal error

Following is a sample Request/Response for submission of a single document:

Request:

```
POST /api/rest/upload HTTP/1.1
Host: www.myhost.com
Content-Type: application/x-www-form-urlencoded
Content-Length: length
clientId=test1&term=PTSD &title=t1&url=u1&content=c1&extern
  alRef=e1&profileId=p1
```

In this example, a provider (a system or an automated process) with the clientID *test1* submits a single document. The provider asks for analysis for PTSD of the document with external ID *e1*; abbreviation *c1* represents the content of the document.

Response:

```
HTTP/1.1 200 OK
Server: Apache-Coyote/1.1
Content-Type: text/xml;charset=utf-8
Content-Length: 139
Connection: close
<response>
<upload id="111" submitted="1" processed="0" analyzed="0"
  dateTime="2011-06-13T11:56:32.895-04:00" />
</response>
```

Real-time response indicates that one document was successfully submitted but that no documents have been processed yet. The response also provides an *uploadID* that can be used to check upload status, as illustrated below.

6.3.3.2   Get Upload Results

Results are obtained by submitting a GET request to a URL having the following format: http://www.myhost.com/api/rest/upload/{id}

id (mandatory)

batch id returned when uploading documents

Request Parameters:

clientKey (mandatory)

string representing anonymous user; assigned by SentiMetrix©

subTerms (optional)

an optional parameter specifying if the constituent signal scores should be returned for each document satisfying the query. If *subTerms* = 1, the scores for each signal are returned; otherwise, just the top-level scores are returned

Return Codes:

200—Success
400—invalid input
403—the account specified is invalid
404—the resource does not exist
500—the server encountered an internal error

Request:

```
GET /api/rest/upload/123?subTerms=1 HTTP/1.1
Host: www.myhost.com
Content-Length: length
```

Example Response:

```
HTTP/1.1 200 OK
Server: Apache-Coyote/1.1
Content-Type: text/xml;charset=utf-8
Content-Length: length
Connection: close

  <result>
    <upload id="111" submitted="1" processed="1" analyzed="34"
dateTime="2011-06-13T11:56:32.895-04:00">
      <terms>
        <term value="PTSD" />
      </terms>
      <documents>
        <document id="2221" externalRef="ref-456">
          <terms>
            <term value="PTSD" score="2">
```

```
            <subterms>
              <subterm value="ptsd_cognitive" score="1" />
              <subterm value="ptsd_behavioral" score="2" />
              <subterm value="ptsd_emotional" score="0" />
              <subterm value="ptsd_physical" score="3" />
              <subterm value="ptsd_functional" score="4" />
            </subterms>
          </term>
        </terms>
      </document>
    </documents>
  </upload>
</result>
```

6.3.3.3   Getting Scores

To retrieve the scores satisfying the query parameters, a GET request is submitted to a URL having the following format: http://www.myhost.com/api/rest/search/scores

Arguments:

clientID (mandatory)

> string representing anonymous user; assigned by SentiMetrix©

fromdate (optional)

> format is yyyy-mm-dd; the starting date of the interval to search for scores; default is 7 days before the todate

todate (optional)

> format is yyyy-mm-dd; the ending date of the interval to search for scores; default is today

language (optional)

> language code(s) to limit the search to; default is English

> > *sources* defines the source data to search

> > > b: blogs
> > > n: news articles
> > > f: forums
> > > c: chat
> > > i interviews
> > > s: Brain Fitness surveys

> > the default is to search all

> > > *query*

> > > the search terms, such as "PTSD"

subterm

> an optional parameter specifying if the constituent signal scores should be returned for each document satisfying the query. If *subterms* = 1, the scores for each signal are returned; otherwise, just the top-level scores are returned

Example Response:

```
<result>
  <query terms="ptsd">
    <scores mean="0.01" volume-"1207">
      <score date="2011-01-30" mean ="-0.007" median="-0.006"
volume="130" />
      <score date="2011-01-31" mean ="-0.001" median="-0.11"
volume="65" />
      <score  date="2011-02-01"  mean  ="0.007"  median="0.05"
volume="90" />
    </scores>
  </query>
</result>
```

6.3.3.4   Getting Documents

To get documents from the API a GET request is submitted to a URL having the following format: http://www.myhost.com/api/rest/search/documents

Arguments:

clientID (mandatory)

> string representing anonymous user; assigned by SentiMetrix©

fromdate (optional)

> format is yyyy-mm-dd; the starting date of the interval to search for scores; default is 7 days before the today

todate (optional)

> format is yyyy-mm-dd; the ending date of the interval to search for scores; default is today

language (optional)

> language code(s) to limit the search to; default is English

> *sources*

> defines the source data to search

> > b: blogs
> > n: news articles

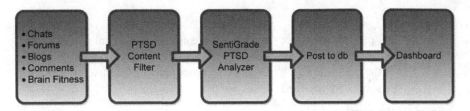

Fig. 6.4 SentiMetrix© data processing pipeline

> f: forums
> c: chat
> i: interviews
> s: Brain Fitness surveys

the default is to search all

query

the search terms

Example Response:
```
<result>
  <query term="ptsd">
    <documents date="2011-04-01">
      <document uid="123456">
        <headline>AfPak: the unwinnable war</headline>
        <url>http://www.myhost.com/article/1</url>
        <score>0.23</score>
        <language>en</language>
        <source>123</source>
      </document>
      <document uid="3456">
        <headline>Many suffering from stress</headline>
        <url>http://www.myhost.com/article/2</url>
        <score>-0.23</score>
        <language>en</language>
        <source>1233</source>
      </document>
    <documents date="2011-04-02">
    </documents>
  </query>
</result>
```

6.3.4   Text Analysis Data Flow

The documents sent through the API go through a processing pipeline depicted in Fig. 6.4.

The first block indicates the source data, which is submitted to the system for processing, and defines a few potential sources for the data.

The Content Filter is built on the Mallet[1] statistical text-processing package. It is a trained classifier whose task is to calculate the likelihood that the document talks about the topic of interest (concepts/syndromes related to PTSD), or is concerned with some other topics. Since the *signatures* corresponding to such topics differ between different source categories (for example, scholarly articles from the Psychological Materials Library use very different language from colloquial terminology one is likely to encounter in a blog or forum post) training on each data source was done separately.

The SentiGrade™ Analyzer is the core SentiGrade™ engine incorporating the TAPIR modifications described in Chap. 4. It performs the deep text analysis and computes the scores for each of the individual psychological signals defined by the PTSD Ontology developed for the project. The resulting scores are stored in a relational database, and are available both for retrieval via the SentiMetrix© API and the SentiMetrix© dashboard.

6.4   Dashboard

The dashboard described here has been developed specifically for the project and differs significantly from the commercially available SentiGrade™ user interface. It is seen as a tool to be used by clinicians or analysts and not by general users. This dashboard preserves the general idea of giving the user the ability to drill down from general high-level results to the individual documents, and presenting the results via time-series charts, plus adds additional functionality and, of course, complexity in an attempt to offer substantial flexibility to the user.

The project SentiMetrix© Analysis dashboard consists of five pages, united by a common look and feel, navigation and available filters. These are described below.

6.4.1   Filters

The Dashboard makes use of a variety of filters to enable viewers to view both the summary and the detailed data:

---

[1] Mallet is a software package. See http://mallet.cs.umass.edu/ for more information.

Fig. 6.5 Filter interface options

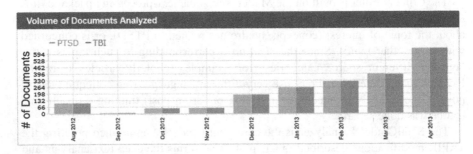

Fig. 6.6 A representative landing page

- Syndrome: Viewer can focus on PTSD or another condition. Default will be PTSD and will remain at *current view* until modified
- Population: System can group anonymous members into a variety of groups. For user testing, groups may include the Control Group, those diagnosed, those being treated, or family members. Going forward, groups could be used for regions, branches of service, etc.
- Source: Indicates *source* of the document. Initial options include Blog, Forums, Blogs, Interview Transcripts, Brain Fitness (text from survey entries), or *All*
- Date Range: Calendar flyovers enable viewer to select date range of single day up to multiple months (Fig. 6.5)

6.4.2   Landing Page

The Landing (Home) page displays general statistics about the documents contained in the system and the volume of occurrences with PTSD signals. This is the first page displayed to any dashboard user with the intended goal of presenting the *at a glance* picture of the data available, including: average, mean and standard deviation of the scores for the overall user population in the specified data range (Fig. 6.6).

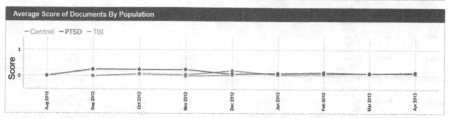

Population Statistics						
Population	Total Number of Documents	Syndrome	Documents Positive for Syndrome	% of Total Documents Positive for Syndrome	Documents with Syndrome Signals	% of Total Documents with Syndrome Signals
PTSD	1085	PTSD	119	10.97 %	426	39.26 %
PTSD	1085	TBI	114	10.51 %	442	40.74 %
TBI	17	PTSD	0	0.00 %	5	29.41 %
TBI	17	TBI	1	5.88 %	5	29.41 %
Control	927	PTSD	93	10.03 %	378	40.78 %
Control	927	TBI	75	8.09 %	392	42.29 %

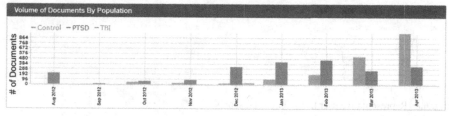

Fig. 6.7 Sample population page

6.4.3 Population Page

The Population page makes it possible to compare different groups of anonymous users within a syndrome. This page is expected to be the common starting point for comparing overall results across populations (Fig. 6.7).

6.4.4 User Listing Page

The User Listing page provides a list of all anonymous users along with their corresponding scores for signals and syndrome. The page displays the anonymous user IDs, population information for each user, and corresponding scores for each of the individual signals averaged over the specified date range. The time of the last update (when the most recent submission from the user has been received) is also displayed. The data can be sorted by any field (Fig. 6.8).

User ID	Populations	Source	Syndrome	Physical	Cognitive	Emotional	Behavioral	Functional	Uploaded At	Actions
user038	Control	Brain Fitness, Forums	PTSD		0.5	0.6			04/29/13 16:51 PDT	Details
user038	Control	Brain Fitness, Forums	TBI		0.5	0.538	0.6	0.5	04/29/13 16:51 PDT	Details
user047	Control	Brain Fitness, Forums	PTSD	0.5	0.533	0.622			04/29/13 15:11 PDT	Details
user047	Control	Brain Fitness, Forums	TBI	0.5	0.5	0.52	0.541	0.5	04/29/13 15:11 PDT	Details
user003	Control	Brain Fitness, Forums	PTSD		0.55	0.525			04/29/13 12:58 PDT	Details
user003	Control	Brain Fitness, Forums	TBI	0.5	0.5	0.514	0.55		04/29/13 12:58 PDT	Details
user075	PTSD	Brain Fitness, Forums	PTSD	0.5	0.525	0.581			04/29/13 11:51 PDT	Details
user075	PTSD	Brain Fitness, Forums	TBI	0.5	0.5	0.541	0.556	0.5	04/29/13 11:51 PDT	Details
user021	Control	Brain Fitness, Forums	PTSD			0.575			04/29/13 11:46 PDT	Details
user021	Control	Brain Fitness, Forums	TBI		0.5	0.533	0.6		04/29/13 11:46 PDT	Details
user022	Control	Brain Fitness, Forums	PTSD			0.5			04/29/13 11:07 PDT	Details
user022	Control	Brain Fitness, Forums	TBI	0.5		0.5	0.567		04/29/13 11:07 PDT	Details

Showing 1 to 20 of 144   << < 1 2 3 4 5 6 7 8 > >>

Fig. 6.8 Representative user listing page and scores

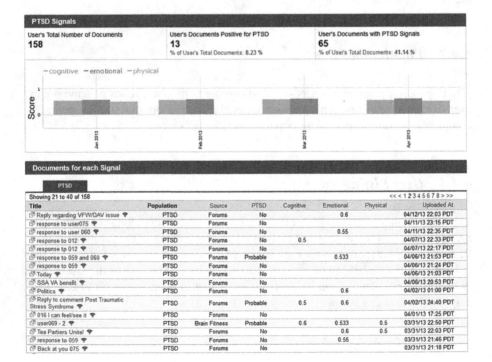

PTSD Signals

User's Total Number of Documents	User's Documents Positive for PTSD	User's Documents with PTSD Signals
158	**13**	**65**
	% of User's Total Documents: 8.23 %	% of User's Total Documents: 41.14 %

— cognitive — emotional — physical

Documents for each Signal

PTSD

Showing 21 to 40 of 158   << < 1 2 3 4 5 6 7 8 > >>

Title	Population	Source	PTSD	Cognitive	Emotional	Physical	Uploaded At
Reply regarding VFW/DAV issue	PTSD	Forums	No		0.6		04/12/13 22:03 PDT
response to user075	PTSD	Forums	No				04/11/13 23:15 PDT
response to user 060	PTSD	Forums	No		0.55		04/11/13 22:35 PDT
response to 012	PTSD	Forums	No	0.5			04/07/13 22:33 PDT
response tp 012	PTSD	Forums	No				04/07/13 22:17 PDT
response to 059 and 060	PTSD	Forums	Probable		0.533		04/06/13 21:53 PDT
response to 059	PTSD	Forums	No				04/06/13 21:24 PDT
Today	PTSD	Forums	No				04/06/13 21:03 PDT
SSA VA benefit	PTSD	Forums	No				04/06/13 20:53 PDT
Politics	PTSD	Forums	No		0.6		04/02/13 01:00 PDT
Reply to comment Post Traumatic Stress Syndrome	PTSD	Forums	Probable	0.5	0.6		04/02/13 24:40 PDT
016 I can feel/see it	PTSD	Forums	No				04/01/13 17:25 PDT
user069 - 2	PTSD	Brain Fitness	Probable	0.6	0.533	0.5	03/31/13 22:50 PDT
Tea Partiers Unite!	PTSD	Forums	No		0.6	0.5	03/31/13 22:03 PDT
response to 059	PTSD	Forums	No		0.55		03/31/13 21:46 PDT
Back at you 075	PTSD	Forums	No				03/31/13 21:18 PDT

Fig. 6.9 Sample user detail page

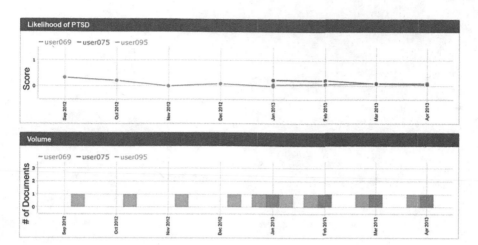

Fig. 6.10 A representative user comparison display, with three users

6.4.5 User Detail Page

The User Detail page is intended to be the primary page for analyzing results of a specific anonymous user. The page presents the bar charts representing the numeric scores for each of the individual signals, for all the syndromes that were detected for the anonymous users. As outlined earlier, the scoring system is discrete, with the values ranging from 0 (never) to 4 (often) denoting the frequency of experience of the corresponding signal. The tabbed listing below the charts lists the scores corresponding to each signal and the links to the original documents from which the scores were calculated (Fig. 6.9).

6.4.6 User Comparison Page

The User Comparison page provides the facilities for comparing up to three anonymous users. The intent is to allow a researcher to look at the comparative dynamics of the users (only selection from the same population is allowed) and explore the reasons for observed differences in trends (Fig. 6.10).

The graphical interface through the SentiMetrix© Dashboard allows for the interactive manipulation of data. For more in-depth analysis of the data and results the environment provides a data export capability, enabling a user to obtain the anonymous data in Comma Separated Value (CSV) format, thus making it possible to import and manipulate the data in a spread sheet application or more enhanced analytical tools. A combination of Dashboard presentation and CSV data will be used to present and analyze the results.

Chapter 7
Conclusions

Abstract The basic hypothesis behind automated data analysis that text data can be used to detect psychological signals—is confirmed by the established statistical methods results presented in the chapter. Text data from discussion forums, interview transcripts and free text questionnaire sections can be subjected to automatic analysis to detect the psychological signals indicating the likelihood of certain syndromes, such as PTSD, in the object of the document, with the results accuracy approaching that of human experts. The chapter discusses the human-annotated data set used for the study, suggests several methods for evaluating the quality of the outcomes, presents the results obtained from validation data and from actual users of the environment, and outlines the directions for future work.

From the statistical analysis standpoint, this chapter presents results of PTSD and Control group difference analyses of variables of interest (e.g., memory, attention, processing speed). The simplest and informative standard characteristics of the variables' (of their distributions) are the mean and standard deviation; the former measuring the central tendency while the latter the scattering (dispersion) around the mean. The properly normalized difference between the sample means, called the (Student) t-statistic, is a standard tool to decide if there is a real difference between the mean values of the variables under study in the two groups. This is done to distinguish from differences in the samples where the difference may be explained by random fluctuations of the variables. In many medical studies the following principle is used: if the value of the t-statistic calculated from the data is such that the probability of getting a larger value when there is no difference in the population means (this probability is called the p-value of the data) is less than 0.05, then the data are considered sufficiently strong evidence for the real difference. In other words, the probability of claiming that there is a real difference when actually there is none (the so called Type I error), is less than 0.05 (i.e., only less than five instances out of 100 will result in the wrong decision).

V. Kagan et al., *Sentiment Analysis for PTSD Signals*, SpringerBriefs in Computer Science,   67
DOI 10.1007/978-1-4614-3097-1_7, © The Author(s) 2013

7.1   Data Set and Human Annotation

For the purposes of this study thousands of documents were harvested from public PTSD-related discussion forums. Based on the likelihood that a small, carefully selected and annotated training set would yield better results compared to using the complete collection of documents, a small-curated subset of 179 documents, hand-picked from several PTSD-related discussion forums, was selected to train the text analysis algorithms. The resulting training set was annotated by a team of psychologists and used to train the text analysis engine. The human annotation (HA) was accomplished through the text-in data-out (TIDO) tool, described in Chap. 4. Learning to use TIDO required little training and the psychologists quickly became effective at using it to annotate documents.

The psychologists were faced with two important issues during the annotation process.

1. Use exclusively the information provided in the text to rate a document. Since the analytical engine only works with the words and sentences present in the documents, any pre-existing knowledge based on intuition, clinical expertise, or other external and non-quantifiable data needed to be discarded by the HA team. A good example of the problem of this kind is the following feedback from the HA team: "… if we feel quite certain a person has had a head trauma and we also believe the person does NOT have PTSD, when we see a symptom (e.g. irritability; exaggerated emotional reactions) that also is on the PTSD list but we don't think the reason the person has the symptom is PTSD, do we mark it on the PTSD list or not?"
2. Take into account solely the evidence that can be discovered by the engine. For example, even if a document mentions that a person was near a powerful explosion (which, to a human analyst, would indicate an elevated likelihood of PTSD) but does not mention any of the PTSD symptoms, the document should have received the HA rating of *unlikely* with regard to PTSD.

To provide a way to mine the expertise of the expert psychologists at some future point, two separate rating categories were introduced. The PTSD_text and PTSD_clinical annotations correspond to the ratings based purely on the text of the document ("think like a computer") and ratings made based on the clinical experience of the psychologists ("as if this were a psychological interview"), respectively.

Only the results of the PTSD_text ratings have been taken into account at this time. Future work may include analyzing results of the PTSD_clinical annotation.

Table 7.1 describes the results of the HA conducted on the 179 documents. The domain of the ratings included L (likely), SL (somewhat likely), U (unlikely) and DK (don't know), reflecting the respective opinion of the annotator with respect to the likelihood of PTSD being present in the object of the text.

There was a relatively large amount of disagreement between the annotators, perhaps due to a high percentage of unrated posts by the Human Annotator 2. As a result, the correlation between the assigned ratings was rather low, with agreement between the annotators occurring in only 77 cases (43 % agreement)

Table 7.1 Documents and respective HA scoring

Rating	HA 1	HA 2
L	12	33
SL	53	22
UL	107	81
DK	3	4
N/R not rated	4	39

Table 7.2 HA aggregated scores

Rating	HA 1	HA 2
Yes	64	52
No	115	127

Table 7.3 HA results based on documents evaluated by all annotators

Rating	HA 1	HA 2
L	6	32
SL	45	21
U	82	79
DK	3	4

Table 7.4 HA aggregates scores based on documents evaluated by all annotators

Rating	HA 1	HA 2
Yes	51	53
No	85	83

The above HA results demonstrate the difficulty in providing a fine-grained judgment to the likelihood of PTSD based on text samples. Since the overarching goal of the project is to develop technologies capable of making binary decisions (likely/not likely to have symptoms indicative of PTSD), a better approach seems to be aggregating the ratings into two larger groups, with L and SL becoming *Yes* and all other ratings set to *No*, as illustrated in Table 7.2. Such conservative grouping avoids *overrating the* likelihood of PTSD.

With this approach, the agreement between the annotators was notably higher, with agreement between the raters occurring in 122 cases (68 %).

When the documents that were rated by only one of the annotators were excluded from consideration, the results for the remaining 136 documents changed to those shown in Table 7.3.

This approach resulted in agreement in 77 cases (56 % agreement) and the aggregated results are shown in Table 7.4 with agreement in 94 cases (69 % agreement) respectively.

Based on the disagreement rate between the raters with respect to the top-level syndrome (PTSD), the analysis of lower-level signals did not seem necessary and was postponed until later stages of the project. Detecting signs of PTSD in textual documents is a hard task for text analytics tools, and it also proved to be a difficult task for the annotators. Since the HA results are the only data representing ground truth at this stage, it clearly made sense to consider the binary outcome (Yes/No) rather than a finer-grained, but less consistent scoring of lower-level signals. The following evaluation approach was used.

7.2 Suggested Evaluation Methodology

Here we outline a method to determine the accuracy of the results from the PTSD engine compared to the *ground truth* as defined by the expert annotators.

1. Suppose we have a set *TS* of *n* documents (*Test Set*) each of which have been scored by *k* human annotators where $k \geq 2$
2. Each human annotator assigns one of four scores U, SU, SL, L standing respectively for *unlikely, somewhat unlikely, somewhat likely, likely*
3. Human annotator *i*'s score, *HS(i,d)* on a document d is *yes* if he scores either SL or L, otherwise it is no
4. Our algorithm returns either *yes* or *no* on each document *d*—this score is denoted by *ALG(d)*
5. The accuracy of annotator *i* with respect to another annotator *j* is defined as follows:

$$Acc(i,j) = \frac{\left|\{d \mid HS(i,d) = yes \ \& \ HS(j,d) = yes\}\right|}{\{d \mid HS(j,d) = yes\}.}.$$

6. We can use the above definition to define the inter-annotator accuracy *i*:

$$Accuracy(i) = \frac{\sum_{j \neq i} Acc(i,j)}{k-1}.$$

7. The accuracy of the human annotators as a whole can now be defined as just the average accuracy of the humans:

$$HumanAcc = \frac{\sum_{i=1}^{k} Accuracy(i)}{k}.$$

8. We can define the accuracy of the algorithm in many ways. The first method says that the algorithm returns a correct answer if it agrees with one of the experts:

$$ALGACC_1 = \frac{\left|\{d \mid ALG(d) = yes \ \& \ (\exists i) \, HS(i,d) = yes\}\right|}{\{d \mid ALG(d) = yes\} \mid}.$$

9. The second definition says the correctness of the algorithm is evaluated in the
same way as the accuracy of the individual human annotators, but is normalized
by the average accuracy of the human annotators. Thus,

$$ALGCOMP(i) = \frac{\left|\{d \quad HS(i,d) = yes \;\&\; ALG(d) = yes\}\right|}{\left|\{d \mid ALG(i,d) = yes\}\right|}.$$

This measure specifies the relative correctness of the algorithm with respect to
human annotator i. To compute an overall accuracy of the algorithm compared to
all human annotators, we use the following formula:

$$ALGACC_2 = \min\left(1, \frac{\frac{\sum_{i=1}^{k} ALGCOMP(i)}{k}}{HumanAcc}\right).$$

The numerator of this formula gives the average accuracy of the algorithm, relative
to the k human annotators. The denominator divides this number by the inter-
human agreement to show how close the algorithm gets to inter-human agreement. It is pretty standard to either show both these numbers side by side or
divide the algorithm accuracy by the human accuracy (as done here) to normalize
the algorithm accuracy by the human accuracy.

7.3   HA Validation Results

Using the above approach, the SentiMetrix© TAPIR results for the binary Yes/No
decision regarding likelihood of PTSD came close to the ratings generated by the
clinical psychologists. A validation set of 359 documents (distinct from the training
set described in Sect. 7.1) was processed by SentiMetrix© and, independently, rated
by three Human Annotators. Using the same approach to the HA ratings, as
described in Sect. 7.1, we considered only the documents where at least two of the
HAs agreed (produced the same rating). There were 347 documents with such *pair-
wise agreement*, and 209 documents where all three HAs agreed on the same rating.
Analysis excluded the documents for which all three annotators produced different
ratings. The results are shown in Table 7.5.

Table 7.5 TAPIR and HA result comparison

TAPIR results compared to	Accuracy
HA pairwise agreement (at least two annotators agreed on a rating)	0.85
HA unanimous agreement (all three annotators agreed on the same rating)	0.88

The results look promising, with the automated analysis of the training set producing results approaching human accuracy.

7.4 User Testing and Results

All the analysis to this point was performed on a data set that was hand-selected from the public PTSD-related forums. Real-world environments involve richer data sets, obtained from actual users participating in forums, chat rooms, blogs and Brain Fitness surveys. For this project, a controlled user testing was performed in order to obtain a richer data set for further evaluating the accuracy of the automated PTSD-related signals detection.

During this next (testing) phase, a group of veterans, recruited by the University of California at Davis (UCD), was screened for PTSD by a group of UCD clinical psychologists; participants were then assigned anonymous IDs to access the testing environment created for the project. These volunteers anonymously interacted in the test environment and the automated text analysis tools will process the content generated. At the end of the testing period, the results of the automated analysis were compared with the PTSD group membership as defined by the psychologists.

The User Test consisted of 89 Veterans anonymously accessing a secure environment, referred to as the Community for Education, Wellness and Support (CEWS). The selection process was conducted by VA system clinical psychologists who reviewed the electronic medical record (EMR) of each potential volunteer, and then conducted a structured interview to determine suitability for the study. Following the psychologist screening, each user was given an anonymous userID, for access to the environment, and *assigned* to one of two groups.

- PTSD—users exhibiting signals of PTSD
- Control—users exhibiting neither PTSD nor TBI signals
  The CEWS consists of two distinct data processing components:
- SA—Sentiment Analysis text analysis engine
- BFT—Brain Fitness Toolkit that is based upon a questionnaire-processing engine

CEWS is effectively a social networking environment consisting of blogs, chats, discussion forums, and the ability to comment on relevant articles. CEWS also prompts users to take the Brain Fitness Survey (part of the BFT). The survey consists of both a multiple-choice questionnaire and a number of free text questions. Users access CEWS, go through the BFT and participate in the social network. CEWS collects the anonymous user-generated data and processes through SA and BFT. The outcomes of the processing can be defined as belonging in three groups, as follows:

- Sentiment Analysis—text analysis scores on user documents obtained from the social network components of the test environment.

- Brain Fitness Questionnaire—scores from the multiple-choice questionnaire from Brain Fitness.
- Brain Fitness Free Text—text analysis scores on the free text questions from the Brain Fitness questionnaire.

The processing performed by SA and BFT created data associated with each anonymous user that contained, at the highest level, an *answer* indicating whether PTSD signals exist:

- PTSD—users exhibiting signals of PTSD
- None—users not exhibiting PTSD signals

In addition, each software product produces more detailed results associated with the scoring of each document or questionnaire. These results were also made available for analysis with the goal being to improve the algorithms in order to more accurately detect signals associated with PTSD.

The results of the data analyses assign anonymous userIDs into the above groups. The accuracy was determined by comparing the group assignments done by the software tools to the assignments initially determined by the psychologists.

Tables 7.6 and 7.7 present the descriptive statistics and results of the group difference analyses for the Brain Fitness and Text Analysis data respectively. The standard measures of central tendency (mean) and variability (standard deviation) for the Control Group and the PTSD Group as well as the results of the group difference analyses are presented. The test statistic to determine whether the difference between two sample means is statistically significant (i.e., not simply chance variability across samples) is the t-test. Results of the independent group t-test are presented as t-scores, standardized measures of the difference between the compared group means. The larger the t-score, the more likely the difference between the group means is not due to sampling variability. In inferential hypothesis testing, this is a dichotomous decision; group means are or are not statistically different. To determine significance, the probability level (alpha or the p-value) is required. An alpha of <0.05 is the most commonly used criterion of significance. This implies that if a difference is significant, there is less than 5 % chance that the group mean difference is spurious or a Type I error. When multiple comparisons are being made, to keep $p<0.05$ constant for each t-test, a conservative correction needs to be applied, the Bonferroni correction (0.05/number of planned comparisons). This makes it significantly more difficult to reject the null hypothesis, but if done, the results are surely representative of the population characteristics (i.e., a real difference). Significant group differences are identified by t-scores followed by an asterisk (*). The final tabular column presents Cohen's d, a standardized measure of the size or effect size of the significant group mean difference. The larger Cohen's d, the larger the size of the difference on a qualitative scale (small/medium/large). Significant, but small group differences have limited utility in real life, while significant and large differences are important.

Table 7.6 Brain Fitness measurement variables and statistics

Variable	Control group M	SD	PTSD group M	SD	t	p	d
Memory	78.57	18.62	48.80	23.42	5.450	0.000*	1.400
Attention	74.57	23.22	39.50	29.19	5.150	0.000*	1.320
Processing Speed	74.53	21.36	55.33	26.06	3.120	0.003	0.805
Executive function	81.03	15.14	62.17	24.83	3.550	0.000*	0.917
Anxiety	62.67	5.34	30.00	26.83	4.450	0.000*	1.140
Stress	48.03	34.22	27.03	32.62	2.430	0.018	0.628
Mood	67.30	22.48	47.43	24.11	3.300	0.002	0.852
Emotional Control	64.47	18.87	44.83	16.46	4.290	0.000*	1.100
Emotional Recognition	74.70	19.97	65.53	18.56	1.840	0.071	0.475
Belief Systems	67.37	19.81	58.53	19.51	1.740	0.087	0.449
Optimistic/Negative Bias	73.03	19.95	43.37	27.13	4.820	0.000*	1.240
Relaxation Response	63.73	23.85	44.13	26.40	3.010	0.004	0.779
Social Interaction	52.73	14.81	46.10	13.86	1.790	0.078	0.462
Alcohol Intake	82.30	20.37	72.63	34.11	1.330	0.188	0.344
Cognitive Stimulation	63.20	22.40	55.23	28.88	1.190	0.237	0.308
Diet	53.40	20.08	50.03	17.96	0.684	0.496	0.176
Motivation	64.03	13.02	67.40	17.77	0.837	0.406	0.216
Physical Activity	53.53	31.96	45.87	34.42	0.894	0.375	0.234
Tobacco Use	77.50	25.72	75.83	19.12	0.285	0.777	0.748
Cardiovascular Disease	98.30	9.31	89.87	24.44	1.770	0.083	0.464
Cholesterol	73.27	29.17	71.60	33.18	0.207	0.837	0.054
Chronic/Medical Conditions	55.03	25.28	39.57	19.46	2.650	0.010	0.695
Diabetes	90.77	18.41	92.80	18.77	0.424	0.673	0.111
Blood Pressure	68.27	29.12	61.87	26.22	0.895	0.375	0.235
Mental Health Conditions	82.27	29.00	47.37	33.15	4.340	0.000*	1.120
Stroke/Transient Ischemic Attack	96.67	18.26	93.33	25.37	0.584	0.561	0.153
Body Mass Index	36.03	21.03	32.30	24.43	0.634	0.528	0.166
Fatigue	65.37	16.67	46.00	25.07	3.520	0.000*	0.924
Functional/Physical Disability	83.27	16.03	69.57	25.27	2.510	0.015	0.659
Sensory Handicap	62.63	37.97	46.73	20.39	2.020	0.048	0.530
Sleep	65.50	17.55	44.60	23.36	3.920	0.000*	1.010

7.4.1 Brain Fitness Analysis Results

Table 7.6 lists the 31 variables measured by the BFT and includes group means, standard deviations (σ), t-scores, alpha levels for all BFT variables and Cohen's *d* values for the variables.

Sixty participants completed the BFT, 30 in the PTSD Group and 30 in the Control Group. This analysis was conducted only on the first administration of the BFT.

Table 7.7 Text Analysis measurement variables and statistics

Variable	Control group M	SD	PTSD group M	SD	t	p	d
PTSD-1	0.129	0.315	0.197	0.373	4.270	0.000*	0.190
PTSD-2	0.087	0.268	0.119	0.304	2.420	0.015	0.111
Cognitive	0.517	0.037	0.527	0.042	1.970	0.049	0.252
Emotional	0.564	0.057	0.571	0.063	1.510	0.131	0.116
Physical	0.504	0.020	0.506	0.025	0.289	0.774	0.088
Anger	0.600	0.065	0.610	0.075	1.550	0.121	0.142
Anxiety	0.568	0.095	0.557	0.019	0.631	0.530	0.160
Startled	0.500	0.000	–	–	–	–	–
Crying	0.511	0.045	0.500	0.000	1.100	0.277	0.345
Depression	0.600	0.000	0.597	0.016	0.958	0.341	0.265
Fear	0.527	0.044	0.529	0.045	0.297	0.767	0.044
Guilt	0.521	0.041	0.571	0.046	3.980	0.000*	1.140
Hallucinations	–	–	–	–	–	0.188	–
Headache	–	–	0.500	0.000	1.190	0.237	–
Hypervigilance	–	–	–	–	–	0.496	–
Insomnia	0.500	0.000	0.500	0.000	–	–	–
Concentration	0.560	0.054	0.550	0.052	0.342	0.738	0.188
Memory Loss	0.500	0.000	0.500	0.000	–	–	–
Nausea	0.500	–	–	–	0.285	0.777	–
Nightmares	–	–	–	–	1.770	0.083	–
Paranoia	0.500	0.000	–	–	0.207	0.837	–
Stress	0.500	0.000	0.500	0.000	2.650	0.010	–
Trauma	0.549	0.053	0.551	0.050	0.284	0.777	0.038
Tremors	0.500	0.000	0.500	0.000	–	–	–

*p < 0.05 Bonferroni corrected
T-scores cannot be computed if at least one of the groups is empty or if the standard deviation
    of both groups is 0

Independent group t-tests were conducted on each of the 31 subscale variables using the quite stringent Bonferroni correction criterion of 0.0016 to hold the alpha level constant at 0.05.

Of the 31 mean differences, nine were significantly different (as indicated by the * in the table), where the PTSD Group was significantly lower on each of the following variables:

- Memory
- Attention
- Anxiety
- Emotional Control
- Optimism/Negativity
- Mental Health Condition
- Sleep
- Executive Function
- Fatigue

Using Cohen's d statistic with pooled variance, all of these significant differences represent quite large effect sizes. These analyses indicate that the PTSD Group manifests significantly more neuropsychological problems, emotional psychopathology, and health-related problems than does the Control Group. By using the most stringent criterion to determine significant differences between the groups' means on each variable, these differences almost certainly reflect clinically significant problems generalizable to the entire military PTSD population.

7.4.1.1   Group Re-classification Analyses

Binary logistic regression analyses were conducted (PASW/SPSS 18.0) to predict participants' actual group membership based exclusively on those BFT variables that had significant group mean differences. The outcome indicates that the BFT is sensitive to identifying PTSD Group membership compared with psychiatric controls.

Using the nine significantly different BFT variables noted above resulted in an improved overall classification hit rate of 85 % (Control Group 86.7 % and PTSD Group 83.3 %). Using the entire subset of 31 variables in the re-classification resulted in a 100 % correct classification rate.

7.4.1.2   BFT Summary Score Analyses

The BFT uses three distinct scoring algorithms for determining existence of PTSD signals. These algorithms were applied to the 39 PCL-M variables measured by the BFT.

PCL, an algorithm which tabulates responses to the PTSD Checklist (PCL), a validated self-report questionnaire[1] for screening, diagnosing and monitoring symptom changes in those undergoing treatment.

BF, an experimental algorithm which tabulates responses to a proprietary, commercially available brain fitness questionnaire (BFT).

SA, the text analysis scores from processing the free text questions of the BFT and detecting PTSD signals in that text.

The three PTSD summary scores were correlated using the Pearson product moment correlational analyses.

$PCL \times BF = 0.66, p < 0.01$
$PCL \times SA = 0.18, p > 0.05$
$BF \times SA = 0.06, p > 0.05$

Using each of these summary scores as the re-classification variable:

PCL: 78.30 % hit rate (96.7 % for Control and 60 % for PTSD)
BF: 73.30 % hit rate (76.7 % for Control and 70 % for PTSD)
SA: 60.00 % hit rate (70 % for Control and 50 % for PTSD)

---

[1] Details about the PCL, the various versions (military, civilian, specific), administration guidelines, scoring methodologies, interpretation and measuring change can be found at the National Center for PTSD site, http://www.ptsd.va.gov/professional/pages/assessments/ptsd-checklist.asp.

Group	PTSD-BIN 0	PTSD-BIN 1
Control	871	96
PTSD	773	124

Table 7.8 Chi-square analysis results

7.4.2   Text Analysis Results

Table 7.7 lists the 22 variables measured by the Text Analysis algorithms and includes group means, standard deviations (σ), t-scores, alpha levels for all text analysis variables and Cohen's d for the variables that are significantly different.

PTSD-1 and PTSD-2 represent the results of two distinct algorithms which use the scores of the 22 variables to compute an overall PTSD score.

Independent group t-tests were conducted on each of the 24 subscale variables using the quite stringent Bonferroni correction criterion of 0.002 to hold the alpha level constant at 0.05.

Of the 24 mean differences, two were significantly different: The PTSD Group was significantly higher on each of the following variables:

- PTSD-1
- Guilt

Using Cohen's d statistic with pooled variance, the effect size for the PTSD-1 variable was in the small range while the difference in guilt was a quite large effect size.

7.4.2.1   Cross Tabulation Analysis: PTSD-BIN

The Text Analysis algorithms also computed one other variable, PTSD-BIN. This results in binary (0 or 1) classification derived from the distinct algorithms that compute an overall PTSD score. The PTSD BIN provides a dichotomous classification to compare with the actual dichotomous group membership. To determine if there is a significant relationship between these nominal level categories requires a Chi-square test of independence.

A Chi-square analysis was conducted to determine the relationship between group membership (Control/PTSD) and the classification using the PTSD-BIN dichotomous score (0/1). There was a significant 2×2 Chi-square$=6.79$, $p=0.0092$ (Table 7.8).

These results indicate that the frequency distributions are not independent. Using this algorithm, most PTSD participants were erroneously assigned to the control group.

7.4.2.2   Group Re-classification Analyses

Binary logistic regression analyses were conducted (PASW/SPSS 18.0) to re-classify participants into their predicted clinical group based exclusively on the two variables whose means were significantly different between the PTSD and Control Groups. The CEWS is sensitive to identifying PTSD Group membership compared with psychiatric controls.

Using the two significantly different CEWS variables resulted in an overall classification hit rate of 73.7 % (Control Group 78.9 % and PTSD Group 71.1 %). The overall hit rate reflects the re-classification accuracy using only those two variables (PTSD-1 and Guilt) as predictors.

A full data set classification analysis was not possible to perform due to too much missing (not calculated) data in the variable scores obtained from the text analysis algorithms. Effectively the scores of the 22 variables represent a sparse matrix, which is not conducive to performing re-classification analysis.

7.5   Future Work

The data generated by the anonymous users during user testing resulted in a richer data set compared to the one used for algorithm training. This would enable for the text processing models to be adjusted to account for variations in documents, which should result in better overall accuracy, since the algorithms have not been tuned to date. Some of the questions, which will need to be answered, include:

- How should the scores calculated from individual documents, from a single data source, be combined to obtain the *user* score
- Should the data from different sources be processed differently
- What is the best way to combine the results obtained from different data sources to compute the overall score for a user

7.5.1   Testing and Analyses

The data collected during the user testing allow for multi-faceted analysis, which will require new models to be developed and considerable time to perform. Of interest is the time component and how a specific user's data may change over time. Multi-source data may provide for new insights into psychological signal detection and the combination of tools and algorithms may lead to higher accuracies.

7.5.1.1   Definitions

There are two components to the data definition, data source and time. Those are defined in the following sections.

Data Source Component

The following definitions define results obtained from the various data sources and are used in the analysis options outlined in the next section:

HA_G	Group assignment of anonymous users done by psychologists based upon EMR review and a clinical screening interview
BFT_{PQ}	Brain fitness toolkit scores for PTSD and group assignment obtained from the processing of the PCL-M checklist
SA_{PBFT}	Sentiment analysis PTSD scores of anonymous user documents and group assignment obtained from the brain fitness toolkit free text questions
SA_{PIT}	Sentiment analysis PTSD scores of anonymous user documents and group assignment obtained from each user's transcribed interview session (one document per user)
SA_{PSN}	Sentiment analysis PTSD scores of anonymous user documents and group assignment obtained from the CEWS social network

Time Component

The time component differs for sentiment analysis and brain fitness. For brain fitness time is defined by how many times an anonymous user completes the questionnaire and submits it for analysis, which during the study was a minimum of one time and a maximum of three times. For sentiment analysis data was produced on a daily basis (a sample), or for each day an anonymous user created at least one document. While participating in this anonymous testing, users may have created multiple documents in a day; additional research will be needed to determine the best algorithm for integrating scores from such postings. The time component is defined as follows:

t_{SA}	The time period (e.g., $[1 \dots n]$), or discrete time *samples* (e.g., $\{1, 5, 6, 8, 17, 23\}$), of the sentiment analysis scores
t_{BFT}	The discrete time *samples* (e.g., $\{1 \dots n\}$) of the brain fitness toolkit scores

where $n \leq N$ and N is the total number of samples.

7.5.1.2   Analyses

The results obtained from the data processing can be combined and analyzed in multiple ways. A number of these options are outlined below and represent the follow-on analysis to be performed on the results obtained from the system, with the goal being to identify the *best* or most accurate method of identifying psychological signals indicative of PTSD.

Analysis Against HA_G

Compare the results of the automated processing and combinations of those results against the HA assignments made by psychologists after the EMR review and a clinical screening.

1. $SA_{PSN}(t_{SA})$ compared to HA_G
2. $SA_{PBFT}(t_{BFT})$ compared to HA_G
3. SA_{PIT} compared to HA_G
4. $BFT_{PQ}(t_{BFT})$ compared to HA_G
5. $f(SA_{PSN}(t_{SA}), SA_{PBFT}(t_{BFT}))$ compared to HA_G
6. $f(BFT_{PQ}(t_{BFT}), SA_{PBFT}(t_{BFT}))$ compared to HA_G
7. $f(SA_{PSN}(t_{SA}), BFT_{PQ}(t_{BFT}))$ compared to HA_G
8. $f(SA_{PSN}(t_{SA}), SA_{PBFT}(t_{BFT}), BFT_{PQ}(t_{BFT}))$ compared to HA_G

where $f()$ defines a function for computing the outcome of its parameters.

Comparison of Tools

Using HA_G as *ground truth*, compare the results of the tools against each other to determine which tool produces a higher accuracy.

Analysis of Tool Combinations

Perform analysis to determine whether increased accuracy could be determined by deploying a combination of tools. Compare the results of the tools, and combinations of those results, against each other to determine which tool or combination produces a higher accuracy. Such comparative analysis includes:

1. $SA_{PSN}(t_{SA})$ compared to $BFT_{PQ}(t_{BFT})$
2. $f(SA_{PSN}(t_{SA}), SA_{PBFT}(t_{BFT}))$ compared to $BFT_{PQ}(t_{BFT})$
3. $SA_{PSN}(t_{SA})$ compared to $f(BFT_{PQ}(t_{BFT}), SA_{PBFT}(t_{BFT}))$
4. $f(SA_{PSN}(t_{SA}), SA_{PBFT}(t_{BFT}))$ compared to $f(BFT_{PQ}(t_{BFT}), SA_{PBFT}(t_{BFT}))$
5. $f(SA_{PSN}(t_{SA}), BFT_{PQ}(t_{BFT}))$ compared to $SA_{PBFT}(t_{BFT})$

where $f()$ defines a function for computing the outcome of its parameters.

Post Hoc Analysis

In addition to using the higher-level results, analysis could be performed using the lower-level signal scores produced by the tools. Thus, for each tool, analyses of summary signals and *detailed* signals may provide insight on whether certain signals or combinations of signals could yield improved results. Also, it may be possible to determine whether *detailed* signals from a combination of tools could improve overall accuracy.

7.6 Concluding Remarks

This book has outlined an approach for applying text analysis techniques to the problem of identifying signals related to PTSD. The initial hypothesis—suggesting that text analysis technologies can be used to provide warning indicators to assist psychologists in detecting early signs of PTSD—involved expert psychologists working side by side with advanced analytical software.

After the sources for the anonymous data were identified, the experts *scored* the documents, providing the *human-annotated* training set on which the software was trained. This work has clearly demonstrated that PTSD analysis is not an exact science. During the Human Annotation process significant variation in how psychologists assessed and annotated data was observed. However, when the evaluation is reduced to a binary *Yes/No* outcome, the variance between psychologists lessens and the resulting training set was used to custom-tune the software. The output of software classification included the *Yes/No* outcome and a set of intensity measures for lower-level signals.

The results of processing validation data sets (distinct from the training set mentioned above) through the software demonstrated the high accuracy of the automated analysis results are closer to those of the psychologists. The agreement between the automated analysis results and those of human experts ranged between high 70 and high 80 %—a very good result for any text analytics study, and an excellent one for a project investigating something as complicated as psychological signals.

These results prove the initial hypothesis—an advanced text analytics engine can be trained to provide fast and accurate results valuable to psychologists working with a large number of potential PTSD sufferers.

User testing, with a small set of users, further demonstrated that text analysis and structured questionnaires could be used to collect data which once analyzed by automated algorithms could provide a fairly accurate determination of the existence of PTSD signals in text. The PTSD Group was significantly different than the Control Group on a number of text analysis and BFT variables. The differences between the groups were quite large and subsequently could be used to predict actual group membership with the accuracy approaching that of human experts. The PTSD Group manifested specific neuropsychological problems, emotional psychopathology, and other health-related problems that alone could be used to identify high risk veterans.

Follow-on research will investigate the use of the granular data collected as part of the study (e.g., the individual signals or groups to examine whether the fidelity of the results can be improved). The combination of tools and results will also be explored to determine whether the text analysis results could be enhanced when combined with those from another tool (e.g., Brain Fitness Toolkit surveys which may offer additional insight into the likelihood of PTSD in individuals). These and other studies will be the focus of follow-on project phases.